STONES
IN
THE SOUL

STONES IN THE SOUL

One Day in the Life of
an American Rabbi

BEN KAMIN

Macmillan Publishing Company
NEW YORK

Collier Macmillan Canada
TORONTO

Maxwell Macmillan International
NEW YORK   OXFORD   SINGAPORE   SYDNEY

Macmillan Publishing Company
866 Third Avenue, New York, New York 10022

Collier Macmillan Canada, Inc.
1200 Eglinton Avenue East, Suite 200
Don Mills, Ontario, M3C 3N1

Library of Congress Cataloging-in-Publication Data
Kamin, Ben.
Stones in the soul : one day in the life of an American rabbi / Ben Kamin.
p.   cm.
ISBN 0-02-560655-7
1. Kamin, Ben.   2. Rabbis—United States—Biography.   3. Rabbis—
United States—Office.   4. Pastoral counseling (Judaism)
I. Title.
BM755.K285A3   1990
296.6'1—dc20   90-30342
CIP

The author gratefully aknowledges the Jewish Publication Society for
permission to excerpt biblical passages from the *Tanakh*.

Macmillan books are available at special discounts for bulk purchases
for sales promotions, premiums, fund-raising, or educational use.
For details, contact:

Special Sales Director
Macmillan Publishing Company
866 Third Avenue
New York, NY 10022

10 9 8 7 6 5 4 3 2 1

Designed by Jack Meserole

PRINTED IN THE UNITED STATES OF AMERICA

Every word is for Cathy.

Contents

Contents

Acknowledgments

This work had its origins as a magazine piece in the *Cleveland Plain Dealer*. I am indebted to my friend, Diane Carman, who edited the magazine at that time, and who saw fit to print a story about a day in the life of a rabbi.

I respect and appreciate Robert B. Semple, Jr.—one of the leading and most distinguished editors at *The New York Times*. Mr. Semple, with insightful and friendly instruction, arranged for the publication of several of my pieces about the American social scene on the *Times*'s op-ed page. He has had more than a little to do with my career as a writer.

Ron Powers, journalist, broadcaster, teacher, conscience, is my mentor and my friend. It is he who admonished me to write a book. His faith in me made the difference. I wish he could be my congregant.

I gratefully acknowledge the support and patience of my literary agent, Cathy Hemming, and the wisdom and high standards of my editor at Macmillan, Philip Turner. Both have become fast friends to me and to my family. To have benefited from their professional counsel would have been treasure enough. In both cases, I am truly blessed.

Not enough can be said about the good fortune I have in serving as senior rabbi at The Temple–Tifereth Israel in Cleveland. My congregants have endowed me with warmth and encouragement. I have been privy to their lives; I am struck each day by their dignity and resilience. It should be noted that, in this book, fictitious names are sometimes used when I relate an incident. However, I have infringed upon the private stories of real people and do not take this privilege for granted.

I am grateful to my staff, particularly Alice Licker—who constantly organized the business of this adventure. Finally, I wish to express hope that my daughters, Sari and Debra, remain as whole and good-natured as they were while I was distracted by the preparation of this book. My wife, Cathy, read every word here with sweet disposition and firm criticism; she remains the well of my rabbinate.

STONES
IN
THE SOUL

Prologue

I T WAS the holiest of mornings, it was the day of days. I rose to the pulpit of the synagogue, however, trembling with fear. Outside the great, round synagogue, the Yom Kippur sun was hanging almost directly over the hall of prayers. For me now, there was trepidation; I was in crisis, and my congregation was about to indulge me.

The sanctuary, colored by the distilled light of so many stained-glass windows, was filled with a thousand souls. Human meditation clung to the ceilings; the deepest secrets of hundreds of generations rose from wooden pews and silently crowded against the sloping marble walls of this old tabernacle.

But even as I stood and looked into the familiar and welcome faces of my congregation, my heart was far away. It was the fall of 1985; I was consumed by thoughts of another synagogue—in Istanbul, Turkey. I had never been to this synagogue, and had never met or known any of its rabbis or worshipers. But this morning, angry with God, I could not let go of my obsession with a distant group of grieving Turkish Jews.

They had been able to come back the day after a massacre. The survivors, the scarred remnants of the congregation Nevei Shalom in Istanbul, returned following the tragedy. What they saw, what they found —just a few weeks before Yom Kippur—were the smoking fragments of the darkest side of Jewish history. Unbelievably and thankfully, I knew that as I stood before my own congregation on this Day of Atonement, our brothers and sisters at Nevei Shalom were gathered in their singed synagogue—still seeking solace.

I prayed that God would do his duty as well, because as far as I was concerned, God had yet to account for the senseless inferno of the Turkish synagogue.

Indeed, I looked to God that Yom Kippur day for some insight, for some clarification. I told my patient congregation that perhaps it was time for almighty God to make known his goodwill for his worshipers. I challenged the sweet God of my childhood and the more complicated deity of my manhood, even as he opened the Book of Judgment, even as he supposedly would make notations in the pages of our lives, to consider a document which we humans submitted for the inspection of the heavenly court of Yom Kippur.

I referred God to the pulpit of the forlorn Nevei Shalom Synagogue of Istanbul. There, just recently, terrorists—the agents of all that is ungodly in this troubled world—had entered and brought down a screaming hour of rage and horror: "Forgive me, dear God, but I cannot quite get over it. . . . Your children had entered the doorways of the synagogue in peace and tranquility; now the deputies of the angel of death bolted these same doors shut to ensure the completion of their terrible work. Across Europe, I imagine, the bones and ashes of the six million of the Holocaust trembled in the broken earth, reluctant and recoiling from the task of receiving more to their company."

My chest was heaving; I recalled my childhood rabbi, a devout man who took the Bible literally. There are those who believe that God actually writes in a Book of Life at the High Holy Days and designates who shall live and who shall die in the coming year. Now I wondered before my congregation, the simple legends of boyhood shattering into the particles of prayer all about me: "God, had you assigned the death penalty to the seven rabbis, my seven colleagues, who were gunned down on the pulpit of Nevei Shalom Synagogue? Had you actually inscribed all twenty-one souls who were lost that sabbath for death?"

It couldn't be! I was enraged at the fundamentalists who now had no defense against the charge that God would, in fact, have to account for the synagogue murders. I wondered about a God, then, who would have murderers as coauthors in a Book of Life. Old and tender ideas, which had sustained my faith in simpler and younger times, were being pounded into the lectern against which I pleaded. I was beating away the innocence of blind piety, I was separating from religious loins which had taken me this far, but could no longer support my spiritual life. Now I confronted God and found my-self eerily in the midst of the deepest moment of prayer of my lifetime.

The "document" which I now placed before God was a torn page from the prayerbook that had apparently been found in the Turkish synagogue after the night-mare had ended. The news dispatches of the terrorist attack had included the information that a single page —its edges scorched—had remained on the bloodied lectern. In the midst of the rubble of murder, the leaf clung to the pulpit like a parchment of love amidst the tractates of hate. The slanted Hebrew letters of this page spoke to me from synagogue to synagogue. The page, the scorched page from the prayerbook, betrayed the surviving words of *kaddish*—the Jewish prayer for the dead.

Now, on this morning of the Day of Atonement, I asked God to accept the scorched page and enter it into the Book of Judgment. For only a book which would bear such a terrible page could truly be divine, because the world that God judges is a real world. If God could integrate such a document into the spiritual world, then I could somehow live with it in my daily life. I had to find a way to enclose that scorched page into God's table of contents, because as horrifying and ungodly and in-explicable as the real world may be, that is how much I need some spiritual intervention.

God would be only for children if the world were safe for children. Freed of childlike beliefs, I am more desperately in need of faith than ever. Killers are stalk-ing synagogues and airports; my contemporaries are dying of cancer; an insidious retrovirus is compromising human love; I need some answers, dear God! I envy the sweet pietists who talk with God, but theirs is not my world, nor that of my congregants.

I don't know anybody in real life who, like Tevye the milkman of the Sholom Aleichem stories, chats with God. Reading modern newspapers and serious periodicals; frequenting shopping malls; being engaged in pseudointellectual conversations over the coffee-of-the-day about the impropriety of gentrification: Who is going to talk with me about God and God's moods?

Meanwhile, what is there to say about God? We seem to have more cataclysmic cards than he has anyway. We can blow up the world ten million times over, we can put every telephone conversation in New Jersey on a single copper fiber, we can warm up dinner in a computerized kitchen via a memory-ready carphone moving through a cybernetic tollbooth. The world according to Tevye the milkman, which is a world that presumes God's overwhelming centrality, has vanished across a cable converter box's transaxial connection.

But then the trouble comes again, the madness against us. And, suddenly, I need more than the relief of quadraphonic stereo or the escape of four-wheel drive. I need answers, or at least comforting. I need confirmation from you, God of my generations, that after all, you still are a factor. Waking up to the news from Istanbul, from Lebanon, from Nicaragua, from Jerusalem, from the war zones of our own American cities—the trouble in the world: all of it brings me to need some kind of spiritual insight. "The world is too much with us," says the Jewish tradition. It seems the more sophisticated we get, *the more we know*, the more we are lonely for something that can't be programmed on a disk.

I came down from the pulpit that day and resumed my duties. I had the privilege of unleashing my anguish in a public place; not every professional enjoys such a luxury. I may have made somebody think, although I certainly brought no comfort to any of the real victims in Istanbul. But I did realize that in confronting God, in even doubting God, I had finally stood up before God as a grown man. In exchange for my anger, I found out why I am a rabbi.

CHAPTER ONE

Morning Light

M Y RABBINIC DIARY begins with a seed
planted some sixty years ago in the Holy Land.

On Rehov Avoda—"Labour Street"—in the old village of Kfar-Saba, Israel, there is a rambling frame
house. The front yard is small, laced with the kind of
shrubbery that manages to survive in desertlike winds.
The backyard, however, is green; quite full. It is com-
forted by the shade of a towering, strapping mulberry
tree. People sit under the tree, drinking lemonade or
iced tea. They talk of politics, of spirituality, of the Bible,
of a world grown much more complicated than this simple yard near the Judean mountains.

The conversation under the tree is animated even as
it is relaxing and satisfying. The mulberry tree stands
over the members of my family, past and present. Its
shade has soothed three generations of aunts, uncles,
one of my grandmothers, cousins, grandchildren.

This is the house where, in 1930, in the British Mandate of Palestine, my father was born. The tree of my father's generations was planted on the day of his birth. My father is gone; the tree survives with his memory. Indeed, the old tree flourishes, bending in the warm winds of my family history. The soil about the ancient backyard on Rehov Avoda is red and rich with experience; its grasses yearn to grow and survive under the hospitable and kindly tree.

My father's mother—my Grandmother Yaffa—would bring out warm and sticky honey pastry to enjoy under the tree. She would interrupt me with some Yiddish admonishment as I studied my fourth-grade history text. The "text" was the Scriptures; I sat in the breeze scented by nearby orange groves and dreamed dreams of the prophet Elijah and the commander Joshua. Light-years away from the culture of shopping malls and instant bank machines that my daughters have now inherited, my childhood world was filled with a sense of nearby history, of biblical heroes who had lived in the very next valley.

Grandmother Yaffa spoke only Yiddish; the lines on her sunburnt face had been carved early by the *shtetl* experience of the Pale between Poland and Russia. She had escaped before Hitler rose, and I sat under the tree studying Torah as living proof.

My uncle, Yaffa's son-in-law, worked with the old woman in her fresh-smelling towel and fabric shop in the village square. It was Uncle Chaim, with bushy moustache and sweet disposition, who chatted with the new Israeli generation of Hebrew speakers in the shop.

Grandmother Yaffa retained her Yiddish for her own contemporaries who told stories and reminisced and sighed in quiet defiance of these more guttural, native-born sabras.

One of my grandmother's friends once answered a question I had put to her. She spoke to me in Yiddish, even though I had addressed her in Hebrew.

"Why are you talking to me in Yiddish?" I asked.

"Because maybe somewhere, Hitler is listening," came the answer. "And I want him to hear the language he tried to choke."

Now, a generation later, the sun sending soft light through the early morning, I walk across the stone entrance of the building where I do most of my work, the synagogue's suburban branch. My parents crossed the ocean; the temple crossed the American inner city and built a new citadel in distant suburbs.

The branch, in Jerusalem-like brick, crisscrossed by wooden planks and tall windows, is the scrubbed successor to its more noble antecedent. The original building—less used, still revered—is relatively silent at its location near downtown Cleveland. Today's families, whose grandparents used to walk to the temple from "the neighborhood," now come and go from the branch in swift and efficient carpool arrangements from a set of townships and contemporary villages with names like Beachwood, Shaker Heights, Solon, Moreland Hills, Pepper Pike.

Now I walk into this suburban complex, a kind of

ecclesiastic franchise; here is the edifice of the Jewish demographic diaspora. It rose in the late 1960s.

But human feelings flow freely about a rabbi, even if his workplace straddles an American freeway and is but moments from a shopping mall. Here, in a corner of greater Cleveland, I still find myself working to keep alive what Hitler tried to choke.

"Rabbi, what do they want from us?"

It was November of 1988, the fiftieth anniversary of *Kristallnacht*, the Night of Broken Glass which marked the official beginning of the Holocaust. And now there were fresh words from Bonn that prompted Jewish anxiety as far away as Beachwood, Ohio: The speaker of the West German parliament was rationalizing the German people's fascination with Adolf Hitler at a public ceremony marking the somber anniversary. Philipp Jenninger resigned the next day in deep regret. But as a rabbi, I had to respond to the indignation, even the residual fears of my congregants. They had just voted in an American presidential election that was not devoid of racial overtones and cultural tensions.

Americans living in the early 1990s may have telephones in their cars, tiered portfolios in their businesses, and reserved berths in their country clubs. But they also have sickness in their families, drug abuse in their schools, corruption in their civil services. I walk into the synagogue branch on any given morning, and before the day is out, I will have conducted the funeral of a parent, the wedding of somebody else's children, an intervention between disputing parties, the naming of a newborn baby. I will counsel the sick and troubled and perhaps even lead people in prayer. Although it is now a suburban phenomenon, like a drive-through restaurant, the synagogue is still a place where people come to learn, pray, and mourn their dead.

In a world of unyielding excesses, I deal with human beings at the point of their limitations. The young professional who had it all winds up dead in a cold wisp of cocaine; I come into a house where successful and prosperous people are now entwined in the throes of helpless grief. A mother has turned to stone. On chairs, across sofas: Faces, arms, shoulders, even legs are interlocked against the family's gaping wound. Cheeks and nostrils spill into each other; a little sister strokes her father's matted hair—who could see this and ever forget? What shall I say to them?

Years ago, somewhere in between my grandmother's honey pastry and my father's oath of American citizenship, I became aware of what the rabbinic tradition instructs: "Life is with people." This simple phrase is my working credo. The rabbinate is the business of human life. I love it so! What remarkable satisfaction I get most every time I am with people, even when, or perhaps *particularly* when, stones fill their souls.

Americans move through life with efficient technology and with an assortment of stress-management and life-style options. But Americans still hurt, like people always will. Suffering is the inevitable exhaust of being human; the rabbi can apply skills and begin the pattern of healing. If you have any sensitivity at all, you can walk into a room where people are suffering and by your very presence ignite a process that turns pain into experience. These moments of give-and-take, and the willingness of people to respond, cannot be recorded on a videotape, or transmitted via a fax machine.

A given day in the life of a rabbi may be more sorrow-laden than others. Forming the flip side of all this are the wondrous occasions of birth, namings, bar and bat mitzvahs, graduations, weddings. But these happy events do not instruct the soul as do the categories of sickness, anguish, mortality. From these I walk away a better-informed husband and father. For the privilege of being present when people are openly feeling, I truly thank God.

But rabbis are people, too, and we are citizens of society. We know pain and we must manage and organize a public posture when our community is affected by a fateful twist in the national scene. I recall, for example, the High Holy Days of 1986. The new Jewish year was arriving with autumn, and it was not enough for me to shake my head at home as I recalled the startling political events of the previous year. An evidently simple American president had ignored the pleas of the Jewish poet-conscience, Elie Wiesel, and was determined to fulfill a visit to a cemetery in Germany where Nazi SS are buried. Why? For what? Meanwhile, would-be presidents, gearing up for 1988, were behaving in ways that prompted my congregants to seek some signal from a rabbi.

America's politics finds its way regularly onto the pulpit of a liberal Jewish congregation. The 1980s produced presidential campaigns during which Jews found themselves beset by racial tensions and by defensiveness about Israel. The American Jewish community continued to vote heavily Democratic, but a new and unsettling ambivalence was discernible. By the close of the decade, a marked rise in anti-Semitic incidents had been documented across America; a troubling decline in Jewish social activism could also have been graphed.

But if the American landscape is my churning and fascinating pulpit, individual people are nevertheless the instigators of my pulpit experience. "We are broken vessels before God," says the tradition. A rabbi cannot always discharge his responsibilities without being deeply affected by the emotional predicaments of the people involved. When I stand in a family's home and they light a memorial candle for someone they have just buried, the heat and smoke of the flame drift into my face also.

"God's work on earth must truly be our own." This remarkable statement was not uttered by any biblical prophet, nor has any rabbi so clearly defined what is one of the most basic philosophies of the Jewish people. Indeed, it was a young Catholic president who exhorted his fellow citizens this way upon the occasion of his inauguration. John F. Kennedy probably did not realize that he was paraphrasing the Jewish sensibility that, in fact, we human beings are partners with God in creating the world.

A seven-day candle lit by a rabbi and a family; an eternal flame ignited by a nation which still needs to grieve and feel and grow: They're the same thing. With that, I offer a rabbinic diary from within the American social scene—the fruit of an old mulberry tree now transplanted.

This morning comes with tears. Early light is spreading across the eastern horizon, breaking gently into the suburbs of the city. A family has lost their patriarch; I prepare to greet them at the synagogue. There is still a touch of night frost in the air as I walk toward the building. An ebony bust of Moses stands silently in the stone courtyard. The Lawgiver is light-years away from Sinai, here in this geographic confluence near Interstate 271, Beachwood Place Mall, a Marriott Inn, and Corky and Lenny's Delicatessen.

The freeway, the shopping plaza, the chain motel, and the eatery are more familiar coordinates to this bereaved family who are now on their way than is the presence of Moses. I suspect that the rituals and practices of grief which I will shortly impose on the approaching children of my late congregant will be remote as well. But the morning light is familiar, and it gives me comfort, because I believe that human life began with light. My work is grounded in a process called Creation. When I succeed, and people are affected by their generations, then the original creation is reflected and validated. The light is my partner. Jews have been affirming this since the beginning of time.

"Let there be light." The Bible attributes this cry to God. The story of the creation of a world in which people live is a story of love. It begins in utter darkness, in the void of universal nothingness. The deity breaks through this deep blackness in a burst of creative imagination. There was nothing, then there was something. The Bible begins with a flash of hope.

There is a significant difference between this view of the first morning and the manner in which other cultures have explained the coming of the world. Aristotle writes of matter which simply always was. The Greek culture, with its marvelous myths, struggled with charismatic gods, heroic kings, and poetic oracles, but nevertheless left the universe to a straight line. It simply was there, an endless amalgam of dust and time. There is no beginning and no end. In between, on a cloud of chance, people and demigods mingle in sublime tension.

The Jews, perhaps less lyrical, mark time. We start with the spirit of God as it "hovered over the face of the waters." In the first place, if matter was floating about in space, even its most remote particles would have some kind of magnetic connection with the presence of God. "The earth was unformed and void": Where the Greeks leave a mass, the Jews see the potential for a world about to be designed. Into the most profound emptiness will now come divine intervention. Who could read this story and not sense a loving purpose?

I feel the echoes of the original creation at Rosh Hashanah. More normally associated with the heavy themes of sin and repentance, Rosh Hashanah is really the birthday of the world. We traditionally believe that this is the anniversary of creation. It is ironic that this

holiday occurs during early autumn; the leaves are falling to the ground, blazing with color, enriching the soil.
The point is that the season is ripe with what will be.
If the autumn is God's hand in nourishing the earth,
the coming spring will herald the fulfilling involvement
of human beings.

The Hebrew word for repentance, *t'shuvah*, actually
means "turning." At the season of the new year, the
Jews believe that people turn their souls over in intro-
spection and meditation. But not only people turn, according to this religion which loves creation so very
much. The birds turn also, and the plants and the beasts,
and the great natural elements of the spheres. The world
is created again; one can smell it in the wet soil and in
the smoky air which delight and inspire the senses. Into
this cycle we mix our prayers and hopes and our deepest
sensibilities about living in this universe.

In North America, it is somewhat of a challenge to
be so moved or even mystified by the symmetry of creation and the holiday of Rosh Hashanah. To get to a
synagogue, one walks or drives through indifferent
neighborhoods where business and commerce continue, uninterested and uninspired by the Jewish celebration of a world renewed. Debuting in pressed and
shining clothing, scrubbed Jews emerge out of the pockets of America's franchised village developments seeking some ancient connection in an air-conditioned hall
of prayer. It is far from the gates of Jerusalem or the
green hills of Galilee.

But the Jews emerge, in the largest throngs of the
year. They come, spread across various emotional cat-

egories. Some step into the synagogue tentatively, even uncomfortably. Another year of spiritual ambivalence has nevertheless yielded to the prevailing sense of theological responsibility. Perhaps someone died this year, and a rabbi intervened. Prayer has a vague attraction; the memory of a more pious father or a saintly mother presses on the businessperson or the buyer or the attorney, and now the Jewish new year offers a watershed of cleansing rites.

Others come, without the provocation of the life cycle. They enter trembling, fully convinced of the presence of holiness in a room of souls. Like me, they feel the earth in the throes of genesis. They feel God's breath in the fall breezes that shake the leaves and whisper of their generations. The fleeting dusk of Rosh Hashanah eve is for them the last night of the "unformed void." In the morning there will be light. In the morning, God breaks through with the reassurance of water and air and terrain. They are like Adam, the first man, who feared the night, and who quivered with dread until God assured him that morning would come.

It was my great-grandfather, old Yitzhak, who told me of Adam and the long night. Saba Yitzhak (which means "Grandfather Isaac") had a long white beard. When I looked into the remarkably blue eyes, which shone like Mediterranean pools from his snowy face, I was gazing into the wrinkled lines of my ancestry. Saba Yitzhak had dug into the soil of Palestine; he was one of the founding grandfathers of my birthplace—the village of Kfar-Saba, which means "village of the grandfathers."

17

"Adam was so frightened," the old man would say as we walked to the wooden synagogue not far from the village market. It was Saturday morning, and Jews were gathering to pray in the land of Solomon and Joshua. The scent of the oranges came across the humid air from the groves nearby. Onions grew wild in little patches. In the distance, tiny minarets poked into the Judean air: the Arab village of Qalqilya, forbidden yet starkly beautiful, loomed under the hills of Samaria. While my great-grandfather spoke about Adam and the night, it seemed that darkness could never come to this sun-drenched, if divided valley.

"The man was scared because God hadn't told him about the night. Adam had just been created. It was the sixth day, and the world was already filled with cattle and birds and fish, and the heavens blazed with light until late in the day. The light had opened the eyes of the man. But now it seemed strangely to fade. The wind was colder. The day began to grow old, and the man began to grow afraid. When the full blackness came on, the man was overcome with an anxiety that filled his skin. God caused the stars to twinkle, but the little lights were not enough to calm the man. Now we know that the stars are little pieces of tomorrow, but the man didn't know that yet back then."

My great-grandfather paused and stroked his beard. He was beyond old, I thought. His beard had once been gray, I was told. Now he had passed with a kind of ethereal wisdom into the category of agelessness. "Remember the days of old, consider the years of ages past," it says in Deuteronomy. "Ask your father, he will inform you, your elders, they will tell you."

Now my ancient forefather looked at me. "I remember when you woke up in the night. You came to your mother and begged for morning light. You were such a child. Only the dawn would comfort you. This is what happened to Adam. He was sleepless all the night, but breathed with relief when the sun's first rays came through on the horizon. Once again, the light opened the eyes of the man. You see, we are all the same; children of today, children of the Bible. God looks after our fears when he makes the world again each morning."

I played with other children in the courtyard as my great-grandfather went inside to the synagogue, to think of Adam and the night, to dream of Moses and all the others who spoke to him in the valleys of Israel.

"A season is set for everything, a time for every experience under heaven." The author of this milestone passage is traditionally thought to be Solomon, the king of ancient Israel, and the son of David. In truth, the writer is unknown, but the essence of this biblical assertion remains profoundly Jewish.

> A time for being born and a time for dying. . . .
> A time for slaying and a time for healing. . . .
> A time for weeping and a time for laughing. . . .
> A time for loving and a time for hating;
> A time for war and a time for peace.

The people who believe that a loving deity specifically broke through the void and spread light also believe that the world, no matter how tumultuous, is invested with some kind of order. For the Jews, time is an element of the good order installed into the universe by the divine spark which yielded the world we inhabit. People live, people die—even inexplicably or by random chance—and it all reflects the original creation. Time is not a component of haphazardness; it is the element that brings understanding to the critical moments of life's cycle. When someone dies, it is the time to die, just as it was once the time for God to send a shaft of light into the waiting, unformed void.

The biblical Book of Ecclesiastes, from which the above verse is taken, is considered by many to be a document whose theme is exasperation. "All is futile" is its opening statement. "Alas, the wise man dies," complains its author cynically, "just like the fool.

"And so I loathed life. For I was distressed by all that goes on under the sun, because everything is futile and pursuit of wind. So, too, I loathed all the wealth that I was gaining under the sun. For I shall leave it to the man who will succeed me—and who knows whether he will be wise or foolish?—and he will control all the wealth that I gained by toil and wisdom under the sun."

This is a lament as old as human nature, yet within the scroll of Ecclesiastes there seems to emerge a certain consolation: "Sow your seed in the morning, and don't hold back your hand in the evening, since you don't know which is going to succeed. . . . How sweet is the light, what a delight for the eyes to behold the sun! Even if a man lives many years, let him enjoy himself in all of them, remembering how many the days of darkness are going to be."

The consolation is that, within creation, light and darkness flow in a cycle that is reassuringly constant. Time makes sense; nothing, therefore, is beyond the capacity and experience of the world "beneath the sun." Indeed, Ecclesiastes sighs: "There is nothing new beneath the sun." One may take this as skepticism; I find it comforting: Whatever happens to me is part of the normal processes of living and growing. New revelations, even fresh shocks—they have been known to humankind long before me, and will happen to others long after me. So I sow my seeds, I take my chances, I aspire to be creative. God intervened long ago to make the world unfold, not unravel.

It began with the light, which brought time with it. Human life may be laden with vanity, yet "a season is set for everything." For the Jews, "let there be light" is the rubric of peace in a world of bewilderment. Our belief in creation is therapy as we struggle in the predicament of finitude. People must die, as surely as night bridges days. If I believe that God started it all, then it's normal, even when it hurts. And so, as I walk to meet with a family whose father and grandfather has passed from them, the breaking dawn reassures me, and I can withstand their fresh pain.

"I thank you, king and life-giver, that you restored my soul to me. . . . Great is your compassion." These are the words of a Jewish folk song which is sung in the morning. There are some who believe that the soul actually takes temporary leave of the body during sleep and is literally reinstalled as we awaken each morning. This is in keeping with the Jewish sensibility that the soul is, in fact, God's property. The soul is contracted to the person at birth; the terms are the experience of human life. God recalls the soul nightly, and human life is re-created with each morning awakening.

This is a legend (though some regard it fundamentally), but it is ultimately a song to creation. How deeply enthralled is Judaism in this business of making and remaking the world! What trust there is between humanity and the great mystery in which we live each day under the sunlight. Somehow, we are certain of the presence of a "divine spark" which ignited the world. This leap of faith reassures us that what God created (including ourselves), God would certainly not just destroy.

Can anyone accept this good-spirited perception of life, and not therefore adjust to virtually anything which life brings upon us? Surely there is some hope always in a world watched over by a designing creator who paints with light. Surely there is comfort living in a cosmos which was born in a divine mind and not in the random implosion of indifferent matter. My great-grandfather's white beard led me to his wisdom; his plot of earth now leads me through time. It's all possible for me because I believe that God decided one morning to capture light in this bottle of a universe.

Sometimes the darkness comes before the morning has even passed. In my rabbinate, I seek to eulogize and bury older people who have fulfilled a ripe age. But children die too, and rabbis are called into hospital lounges, into living rooms, even into the streets where parents and siblings are suddenly confronted with their greatest horror. This too has to fit somewhere under the sun.

I recall the beautiful spirit of a teenager named Lisa. Lisa was a fifteen-year-old girl who wore an elegant white dress to a sophomore dance. Lisa's doelike eyes always gave out hope; the purplish tone of her young skin betrayed a congenital heart problem which doctors in Toronto sought to correct. It was the same year the fancy rented limousine came to pick up Lisa in the pretty white dress to take her and her friend to the big dance.

I had worried about this sweet youngster who often had difficulty breathing. Softly, her mother revealed to me one day, "You know, Lisa is a special child." I was but a couple of years in the rabbinate then; the many categories of death had been scarcely revealed to me. My own first child had been recently born; little ones were about beginnings, not endings. Alas, rabbis cannot learn from the safe house of Talmud like we learn from the substance of human life.

It was the springtime, and Lisa was preparing for surgery to correct her cardiac difficulty. The operation would take place in Toronto's Hospital for Sick Children. I could barely walk the halls of "Sick Kids"; the sight of babies with lymphoma and adolescents with bullet wounds still knocks my soul out of its pocket. But where there are children, there are miracles. We were all sure of one when it came to Lisa.

I phoned her the night before the surgery and insisted she complete her homework from confirmation class. She was my student as well as my little bird. Lisa had giggled with delight at the recognition of the routine I wished to impose upon her. My admonition proved things would be normal.

I answered the phone at home the next afternoon. The administrator of Temple Sinai in Toronto, where I was the rabbi, spoke to me in a frightened whisper; we were both young fathers and a certain primal dread crackled across the phone lines.

"Lisa died."

I heard his words, but not the idea. "In the name of God, what?"

"She died, on the table."

I looked around the empty dining room in which I sat. The faces of Lisa's parents swept by the windows. My wife and daughter were not at home. When bad news comes, why do we think so much of ourselves? But I truly meant it when I then said to the administrator on the line: "Oh, God, I wish I wasn't alone here right now!"

We buried Lisa in the field of graves under cold sunshine. Her only sibling, Andrew, said the memorial prayer over the freshly turned soil, the Aramaic phrases breaking from his wretched body like torn pages from an ancient scroll. The young man spilled his grief so freely that I felt even the sun had seen something new, after all. Lisa's mother, her empty womb turned asunder, stifled her gasps in controlled measure. An English-woman of great dignity, she immediately became the prevailing support for the two surviving males. Lisa's father was inconsolable, and retains to this day a shadow in his long, Hungarian face.

But the world of God is the sum of its parts, never-theless. Six years later, I stood under a canopy with Lisa's brother, and her parents, and Andrew's new bride. Forever changed, Lisa's family could celebrate nevertheless, as the young boy who cried in the field now stood up as a strapping groom. We heal, somehow; the life cycle reassures with the turning of private sea-sons. Now, there was music, and joy, and certainly memory. But most of all, the wisdom of the rabbinic literature, which spoke especially this new day to a deeply affected family: "God creates new worlds con-stantly by causing marriages to take place."

When the morning comes, dear great-grandfather, I am strong again.

CHAPTER TWO

Human Feelings

GOOD MORNING, Rabbi; we're all here."

I see a great deal of the father in the son who now stands before me. The fifty-seven-year-old attorney who greets me has the same strong jaw, the pale eyes, and quiet demeanor of the sweet old man who finally died two mornings ago. The generations flow through us, I think, as a second son comes through the door, followed by the wives of these two men.

The father was one of the veteran ushers of the temple. One of those congregants upon whom a synagogue truly relies, the octogenarian had volunteered his time to the congregation for a half century. I genuinely liked him; he maintained a broad smile and an engaging personality. I visited him regularly in the hospital after the debilitating stroke came and took the life and flow from the nice man's eyes.

"Abe," I had whispered to him in the white room

with the silent intravenous tubes and unfeeling monitors cluttered about his evaporating essence. "Abe, if you know I'm here, squeeze my hand. My hand is in your hand."

Nothing. A nurse walked in and drew the curtains against the afternoon light. Abe's eyes were open but hollow. The monitors hissed at me in the shadows: green cybernetic serpents. I left the room, feeling helpless.

Now Abe's family sits with me in my study. As it happens a lot, death has come as a relief to them. So often, people wish to clarify that with me, making sure it is all right to feel grateful that the struggle is over. I assure them that there comes a time when death is the only answer. "A time for being born, and a time for dying." Now it is the time to rebuild lives, to try and heal each other with the processes of memory.

But it also important to bury somebody as himself. This soft admonishment—the message of a basic Jewish instinct—is usually well received by the family. It is an early plunge for me in most every eulogy session. This morning, Abe's older son responds: "That seems right, Rabbi. My dad was really very simple. He just loved his family, he just wanted my brother and me to be happy."

Tears are flowing for this successful middle-aged litigator. Feelings are breaking forth against the brick walls of my office in this suburban house of prayers. Looking into the man's glistening eyes, I see a brief flicker of what Abe's hollow eyes lost a few days ago in the white room with the cold monitors. Sons and fathers, I think to myself, suddenly strangely elated about life and its mysterious ability to replenish itself through human generations.

Tears drip onto the carpeting, and suddenly a certain, fragile wave of relief penetrates the room. My great-grandfather's white beard flashes into my eyes. Saba Yitzhak is walking with me in the old village, and again he is telling me about Adam. This time, however, it is about Adam and the first tears spilled by humankind.

It seems as though Adam and Eve—the male and female composites of early humanity—had lost their right to the garden. Eden was a perfect place; it offered God's first partners ecological balance and natural comforts. Built into the lease were a number of requirements and several prohibitions. Judaism and Christianity certainly agree that the man and the woman eventually violated the trust by eating from a certain fruit tree and by being evasive about it. (In fact, Judaism is less interested than Christianity in the idea that Adam and Eve had been evil. Judaism is more intrigued that—by eating from a tree of knowledge—the husband and wife had acted essentially human.)

It seems inevitable: A seductive serpent plus the element of human curiosity would lead to the fall of Adam and Eve. Judaism not only allows for the inclination of people to seek out what is apparently beyond our reach, it actually acknowledges the darker side of human nature as a necessary partner to the good inclination in order to create the category of wisdom. Adam and Eve didn't sin; they grew up. In realizing they were naked, and in reaching for some clothing, they moved from innocence to worldliness. But that doesn't mean they were not devastated to leave paradise.

The rabbinical literature, evolving over time to comment upon the text of scripture, uses the occasion of Adam and Eve's pain in order to explain human tears. The legend, as my Saba Yitzhak once told me, is that the two evicted humans were bereft. The garden had been home, and it had offered them an environment of safety and self-sufficiency. An unknown world lay beyond; what was worse, they were now possessed of some knowledge. Reality caved in upon them, and a powerful dosage of homesickness. The rabbinic legend tells it that the two choked on their despair and loneliness. They were unable to deal with their regret and sadness. They pleaded to God for help.

God was compassionate, although he could not restore Adam and Eve to Eden. But he could give to his human beings a mechanism with which to release grief. God endowed their eyes with tears so that they could cry. And when they cried, they felt some expression. Their unfulfilled gasps turned to therapeutic sobbing. They were able to move on. For the Jews, tears are the salty waters of human experience and knowledge.

Now, the children of my congregant Abe weep in my office. They are possessed of new knowledge and are leaving behind the paradise of childhood forever. On this morning, I am heartened to see that these middle-aged corporate types have not been so hardened by the late twentieth century that they cannot express their grief. I can be satisfied, again, that my tradition believes in human feelings. It is so against emotional constraints—for men as well as women—that the biblical text itself offers a remarkable illustration of demonstrativeness. While my grieving congregrants remember their Abraham, I think of the biblical Abraham.

In his old age, the biblical Abraham was widowed. The father of both Judaism and Islam was nevertheless a feeling and thinking family man who came to parenthood late in life, and who suffered what psychologists consider to be the single most devastating loss— that of one's spouse. Abraham and Sarah had undergone much together: They had been uprooted from their native Mesopotamia and relocated in the promised land of Canaan; they had endured through Sarah's long infertility; they had known long periods of separation from each other. The biblical text even betrays certain tensions that simmered between them, even as any long relationship is rippled by the strains of human experience. But in the end, the story of Abraham and Sarah was a story of love. I find this poignancy to be more significant than any account of miraculous or supernatural happenings associated with these two ancestors of the Jewish people.

The Bible is clear and direct: In the twenty-third chapter of Genesis, it says "Sarah died." Then, one phrase later: "Abraham proceeded to mourn for Sarah and to bewail her." The same Bible which preoccupies itself with many grand events, such as great plagues or celestial displays of fire and smoke, now describes with simple delicacy what would perhaps seem obvious to the reader. An old man is overcome by having lost his wife and breaks down. Yet do we take this necessity for granted, or do we perhaps get some caring direction from such a biblical scenario? Our heroes sometimes take part in miracles; they more likely (like us) take part in the quiet passage of generations.

In fact, the Bible takes pains to point out to us that Abraham was deeply affected by the loss of his beloved. It suggests to us that, in order to deal with grief, one should undertake a process of mourning and remembering, and one should certainly cry. The Bible is a library of human feelings certainly as much as it is a catalog of wonders. Its therapeutic insights about the necessity for grief and its love for life as an experience long predate the contemporary dynamics of self-help groups and stress-management seminars.

The relationship of Abraham and Sarah forms a constant backdrop for me as I deal with a family passing through their generations. If we truly remember people as themselves, then I gain insights in my work by defining my biblical exemplars as individuals with sentiments and with flaws. It is my conviction that this is why the biblical literature is so enduring. I don't know if it was or was not written by God, or by people directly affected by God. But I do know that the living qualities of its characters are as fascinating as they are discernible. The heroes of this literature are just people; they love, they give birth, they commit crimes, they delight and anger one another. They are imperfect, and, as such, make it possible for us to relate to them. Ultimately, they are not deities; nor are we, as we live and die.

The diaries of Abraham and Sarah, like the accounts

of so many other biblical characters, are the stories of private breakthroughs. Abraham was a man, a husband, and a father. We like to label him as a patriarch; chances are that he thought of himself more simply as somebody's grandfather. Like most people, he had tender attachments to home. Whoever eventually eulogized the biblical Abraham may have noted this characteristic, for the account suggests it with psychological acuity.

Early in Genesis, God conveys a mission to the emerging Abraham. God is quoted as saying to the man: "Go forth from your country, from your community, and from your father's house to the land that I will show you." In my rabbinate, I have rarely met a successful person who did not undertake some kind of difficult, uprooting journey in his or her lifetime. But in laying out the dynamic of Abraham's watershed passage, the Bible could be cited for presenting the sequence backwards.

On the surface, it might appear that the order for Abraham's departure pattern is in reverse. The text says: "from your country, from your community, and from your father's house." But when a person undertakes an international journey, the unfolding dynamic is not country, town, and then house. You normally leave the other way around.

I daresay that when I travel to Europe or Israel, I leave my home first, my metropolitan community next, and then, via air or sea, I depart my country. But the Bible is more interested in human feelings than it is in correct geographics. When you have to leave somewhere, especially if you have to "go forth" and begin some new and challenging enterprise, the leaving is really measured in the qualities of attachment.

The truth is that even though "your country" is mentioned first in Abraham's exit charge, you really have the least emotional difficulty separating from your national framework—the country. You then have the second greatest difficulty in separating from your town, your city—the streets and storefronts and other local landmarks which have been familiar and reassuring to you perhaps since childhood.

But the Bible, a book of sentiments, knows that the greatest difficulty—even as you pass through this door first in the process of life's "going forth"—is leaving your father and mother's house. Suddenly, the seemingly benign verse about Abraham's passage to a new life is laden with psychological meaning, especially in its carefully stated order.

No journey is more primary than leaving the home of your generations. Certainly, you may pass this threshold first, but you forget it last, if ever. The kitchen table where you and your family talked and planned and dreamed; the backyard where you played and fantasized; the bedroom where you drifted off to sleep at night, where memories and secrets lie in old drawers and closets—these are the geographic elements of the soul.

Yes, you go out of here first, and you leave your city second, and your national boundary last. But the Bible knows the truth. Abraham truly did leave his country behind first, his village second, and he let loose his grasp on his own house last. That is how people deal with passages, because when God made people his partners in creation, God also endowed us with affections.

The Bible routinely weaves the quiet circumstances of human love in and out of the greater chronicles it describes. Love is not always perfect or even redeeming; neither are the biblical characters upon whom love makes its impact. Jacob loved Joseph so very much (more than all his children, because he was the son of his old age) that Jacob's other sons were driven to insane jealousy. The Bible tells us straight: Jacob was shameless in his favoritism. While the other sons were busy tending to the family's sheep, Joseph paraded about with a multicolored coat given to him by his father. Joseph was only seventeen at the time; can an adolescent be responsible if the parent is so shortsighted? Joseph's brothers eventually attempted fratricide after Joseph's conceit and taunting had become too much for the others to bear. Could the Bible be more realistic in telling us the story of such family stress? The early accounts of Jacob and his offspring may be found in the case files of most any contemporary psychology group practice. The Bible may be old, but not older than the emotional labyrinth of love/hate.

I see parents hurting their kids; the bruises are not always physically evident. I try to be patient with young people who won't stop clinging to me, their eyes empty of light, their breath unfamiliar, their mannerisms strange, their whining, yearning need *to be noticed* sometimes too much for me to bear. When love is unevenly distributed, or simply held aloof, it burns off the soft edges of young hearts. Indifference neutralizes the creative instincts of teenagers; they drift off into shopping centers, punching aimlessly into game machines and coupon dispensers. They have access to many material things: lightweight earphones, Nintendo units, cellular phones, microwaveable TV dinners. But so many of them are raked by neglect, so many are yielding silent screams of agony.

When I come home to my two little daughters, I often find myself unable to let go of them. Sari and Debra, both born in the 1980s, are good-natured kids who inherit their mother's considerable tolerance and some measure of my emotional crosswinds. Growing into this mall culture whose opposite coordinates are Cosby and crack, my children are nevertheless tiny social workers for me as I come in and out of the maelstrom of rabbinic involvement. I can only come home to my own babies and practically inhale their sweet cheeks and their warm flesh and their pH-balanced thick hair. I'll surrender them to the right kind of designer sneakers, I'll release them reluctantly to a schoolbus full of elementary school hotshots already afflicted with eye shadow and pierced ears and heavy-metal language, but I will not give them up to a civilization too programmed for tenderness. Nor will I accept the more clinical framework of family life so righteously demanded by the new verities of double income and day care. No matter who watches my children from time to time, I am not "bonded" to them; I just love them.

They reward me with feelings returned, and I go back to the needy children of so many encounters, to the overwhelmed parents of so many broken situations with that much more solicitude. The Bible characters speak to me, and my living family kisses me with the instinct for patience. "We are broken vessels before God," my tradition reiterates. Simply put, we are as human as the feelings that bend our souls and either destroy us or inform us. I plead for spirituality in an era of hardboiled investment seminars; I plead for imagination at a time when kids know too much even to imagine.

"Good morning, Rabbi; we're all here."

So begins the eulogy session in my office; in this case, emotions will fill up the air healthfully and even beautifully. This family always could have said, "We're all here." These children and their own children have carefully maintained the milestones of their lives. They have named their offspring at birth with ceremony, they have blessed them at graduations, they have surrendered them with sprinkling eyes to the wedding canopies. The death of their patriarch, Abe, had come in its time like the shaft of light had come in its time to start the whole process. Fortunate that Abe had been given eighty years, even more fortunate that life had been cherished with dignity, that these descendants could come to this juncture and represent their sentiments perfectly in the ancient verse from Genesis: "And Abraham died at a good ripe age, old and contented."

Abe had seven grandchildren. I speak to his two sons and their wives now with me in the office. We have gone through a series of perfunctory recitations: Abe was born in Cleveland and was graduated from East Technical High School. He had garnered a few civic awards, and had enjoyed a long career with the White Sewing Machine Company. All these biographical notes will be published in the newspaper obituary, and I will allude to them in the spoken eulogy. But now I say, "It agreed with him to be a grandfather, didn't it?"

The Book of Life is open; Abe's sons begin to inscribe.

CHAPTER THREE

Sons and Fathers

ABE'S SONS, Lewis and Richard, both let out soft laughs. Laughter in such a session may signify relief, even pleasure. It sometimes, however, signals an element of discomfort; it can, in fact, be the soul clearing its throat. Lewis is five years older than Richard, and even now they appear to be big and little brother. Their wives, both pretty, both polite, exchange quick glances.

"When my dad was with my kids," says Abe's older son, "it was like he was young again. I mean, frankly, he spent time with me and with my wife really only in the presence of our children. They would come to us— he and my mom—or we would come to them. But it was my kids, and my brother's kids. We talked much more about them, their needs, their schools, their clothes, their *everything*, than we did about anything else."

The other son appears restless, and looks at his wife

as he speaks. "He really didn't want to be a grandfather at first, don't you agree, Lew? Remember?" Richard's face is full of feeling, he is recalling something very genuine which he and his brother evidently do not address very often.

"Well, he was okay by the time your kids came along," says Lewis. I think there is a trace of the bitter in his voice, and I take a breath in slowly. While I prefer peace in the session, I am not about to interrupt the unfolding set of concerns. I take notes as people remember, but now I am not writing on my pad.

"No, no," says Richard, truly wishing to convey something. "You've always thought that, but it had nothing to do with your kids or my kids or anything like that. Look, you were married first, and you were just in your early twenties. So what was Dad, about fifty-five?"

"He was fifty-three when I married Janis." Lewis' voice is calm; he is not looking for trouble. I breathe out again.

"Okay, fifty-three," says Richard. "So he was almost sixty when I got married. At fifty-three, he was really robust, really in his prime." The little brother is talking to me again, but Lewis is listening very carefully. "My father did not want to grow old. He took a lot of pride in himself. When my brother got married, we all understood that—even though Abe loved Janis—it was some kind of passage for him. It meant his own life was moving along."

Now I ask, "What do you mean, exactly? What was happening, Lew and Janis?" I want to hear from the wives, and I am also wondering why these middle-aged children have elected not to bring Abe's widow along for this session.

But the women will not interrupt. Lewis looks at me with kindness. I really know him better than any of the others; he has been the most visible at the hospital during Abe's final weeks and days. I remember the first time I had visited the old usher following the stroke that had at last silenced him. Lewis somewhat startled me as I emerged from the scrubbed room in Mount Sinai Hospital. I thought I had been alone with Abe.

"Rabbi, thank you for coming," Lewis had said to me. "There's not much that can be done for Dad anymore. But I appreciate your being here and what you have been doing."

I think: What a soft, even-tempered man. Pleasantly lean with gentle lines, and wearing ivory shirt sleeves, Lewis strikes me as a man who has succeeded at life and will now succeed quietly with the business of death. A few years earlier, I might have felt critical and righteous if a man did not show emotion at such a time. Now I know enough to let people be themselves. Lewis has dignity, I think; I feel a certain inadequacy next to his restrained capacity. I want very much to please him, and I truly liked his father.

Lewis has said relatively little in this early morning eulogy session. Yet his presence has controlled the meeting. The younger brother, eager and generous, seems committed to creating a family picture that will particularly honor the sensibilities of his sibling; in a strange way, I relate to Richard's desire to satisfy Lewis.

And yet, Lewis is not doing anything to extract such tribute, nor is it his nature to be so demanding. He is just so composed, so reconciled, that he unwittingly has aroused sympathy from me, deference from his brother, and silence from the two wives who occupy their seats like props.

Now Lewis says, "My father had no problem being a grandfather. He was absolutely suited to be one. But, like everything that happened to him, he had a way of, well, growing into a situation. When things were new, they were complicated for him. You didn't know him well enough to see this, Rabbi. You knew him in his final years; everything was settled with him, and he really finished it all happily. But when my first child was born, he came to see me and Janis, and he said, 'So, you had to make me a grandfather already? You had to make me old so fast?' I think it bothered Janis a little, and it kind of hung in there for a while, maybe."

A strange sensation goes through me while a brief silence hangs in my study. *My goodness, Lewis was groping a little*, I think. The neat attorney with the tailored collar is sifting through a layer of emotions and putting it all into an appropriate perspective. While the younger brother appears to relax at this, I find a sense of pleasure. So very fond of Lewis, I now enjoy his humanizing moment.

I stick out my confidence: "Janis felt some resentment? Maybe you did too, Lew?"

"Yes, I did," he says. It is matter-of-fact and crisp. "But I don't think that was particularly abnormal, and it's not been with us for a very long time. Look, I'll be

41

a grandfather soon myself, and so will he." Lewis is looking at his kid brother, the lines on his handsome face curling with knowledge: "I'll feel the way my dad did when my first grandchild arrives; who doesn't? It makes you feel so warm inside, seeing your first grandchild. But it makes you suddenly realize how much time has come and gone. You know, I really was upset with my dad when he told us we shouldn't have made him old with grandchildren. Yes, I was upset, because he said this to Janis. My wife had carried the child; she didn't need to be told off. But now that I'm a middle-aged fellow, I think what my dad went through—even though it caused a strain on us for a while—I think it helped prepare me for the same little crisis. Anyway, it wasn't so bad for him."

Finally, a sound comes from Janis. "Wasn't so bad?" She pulls her head back, releasing something pent-up. Janis uses beautiful, silky hands to pull back thick curls of frosted hair while she speaks. Her face is youthful and uncomplicated; she is appealing and one wants to hear what she has to offer. She looks at me now, and I take my pen in hand, drawing close to the waiting pad.

"My father-in-law loved his sons, loved his grandchildren, loved life itself. Lewis and Richard do things now with their families practically every day that reflect what their dad means to them.

"What about the storytelling, Lew? Why did you love reading to the kids when they were little? What did you *tell* them was the reason you read? If you think Abe had a hard time accepting his age at first, okay, he did. Whatever he said to me then he more than made up for many times over in what he said and did for us and his grandchildren."

"It's true," says Lewis. "Rabbi, my oldest daughter, Melanie, has a collection of bound storybooks which I used to read to her. She and her husband have them now, in their home. I read them to her when she was little. My father had read them to me—"

The crack goes through Lewis like the sound of a punctured balloon. The attorney heaves, fresh grief plummeting from his brow in anguished relief. Janis reaches for him, as the other two sit frozen in memories. The other woman, Leah, much younger, seems uncomfortable. Richard's eyes, never completely dry in this session, now sting him as he wipes away drops from his own lips. I feel my own soul tugged, and I wonder how I will react one day, when Sari or Debra present me with the living testimony of my own advancing generations. My own father did not do well in this category.

It was the early spring of 1976, in Cincinnati, and I looked into the bathroom mirror. The one black suit I owned hung upon me in despair. Such suits are now practically uniforms of my trade, along with automobiles and other personal effects which are appropriately restrained in appearance. But on this March morning, the solitary dark suit was the deeply personal garment of my own new predicament: I was about to attend my very first funeral; my father had dropped dead of a massive infarction the night before. At twenty-three years of age, I had escaped the immediacy of any funerals. My ancestors had been dying off back in Israel; I had read and written tributes in salt-stained international aerograms which had cost me not much more than the price of postage.

Already a rabbinical student, I possessed, until this wretched time, little knowledge of the dead. My training was moving quickly now, from the musty classrooms of Cincinnati's Hebrew Union College into the clear air of experience. My father had taught me a few things while living. But nothing he would transmit gave me more insight than his dying.

Death closes off the ongoing business of the world; in the spring of my father's sudden demise, America was unfolding the banners and toll-free commercial offers of our national bicentennial. On the morning of his funeral, I looked into the mirror and forgot about my father's growing impatience with the marketing of his country's history. For my father, immigrant citizen of the 1960s, love of country was something special. My father drove a Chevy, and he would place a Coca-Cola in the refrigerator like a patriot. But now, the jingles of jingoism and the songs of super-savings had fallen silent. My father lay dead in a box at Weil Funeral Home, and I would shortly have to confront that. Not one person who comes to me now, their mother or father also fettered by time, is deprived of what I learned that day and every day since.

Now, why do I recall my father so particularly as I sit and speak with Lewis and Richard about their father? Certainly, a general association is inevitable; regardless of age, we are forever somebody's child. I am some twenty years younger than my congregant, Lewis, and I have limited knowledge of his professional and social worlds. But we have something in common: Our fathers have both died, and our fathers both expressed, at some time, a fear of aging and grandparenting.

"Don't make me into a grandfather!"

I had just recently told my parents of my intention to marry Cathy; my parents were still very young, in their midforties. It was not so easy for my active, virile father to pour this development into his cup of life. He had been a collegiate soccer player of some renown, and a decorated veteran of Israel's Independence War of 1948–1949. He arrived in America, mastered the English language as well as the engineering sciences. He furthered his education at night, learning aerodynamics and eventually fulfilled his immigrant dream by working as a safety engineer for the "government" of the United States, as he proudly stated. Now, who was coming along, bending the twigs under the forest-bed of my father's personal orchard? It was me, walking on up, tracking the mud from my great-grandfather's plot of earth, unwittingly drawing to a close the many heady years of my father's brave flight across two continents. There was never any question that my father loved me and that I loved and admired him as well; there was no doubt he would fight off the encroachments on his youth that my own life span might bring. So now he said, with thick Semitic intonation: "Don't make me into a grandfather!" The popular wisdom that grandchildren are always greeted with delight oversimplifies the accompanying ambivalence which sometimes needs to be confronted.

Who makes whom into anything? I understand the midlife crises of men and women I meet, but I don't necessarily excuse the tendency to place responsibility for the condition upon the heads of offspring. Possessed of my belief in the breakthrough light of creation, I am inclined to view human life as an evolving process. After my father died, I found out that men in their forties and fifties can have real trouble coping with such things as receding hair, spreading middles, blurred vision, impotence, and the threat of little descendants. Visiting heart attack victims in hospital following the loss of my father, I was shaken to discover just how emotionally weak were many of the men who were the Midwestern-sounding clones of my troubled and departed dad. I also live on with the feeling that—had I known then what I have learned now from involvement with so many other people's families—I might have been able to help my father. But rabbis are like anybody else: We find things out when they happen.

I remember one gentleman whom I visited in the months after losing my father. I was a volunteer chaplain at Cincinnati's Jewish Hospital. The Bicentennial was on in full strength now, without my father's immigrant enthusiasm. Mr. Washofsky was foreign-sounding like my father, which was probably one of the reasons I sought to spend time with him.

"So who are you?" said the sixtyish man, whose pale complexion and white hair made him look even older.

His eyes were deep and shiny, however; they invited me in.

"I'm a student rabbi, Mr. Washofsky. From the Hebrew Union College. I came to visit you." Making note that it was midafternoon on a Friday, I added, "And to wish you a good sabbath."

"A rabbi, eh? You look like a kid." The man shifted his weight in his bed. The tubes in his nose fluttered about as he lifted himself up a bit to give me a closer look. "Yeah, you're a kid. A kid like you back in Warsaw would be pulling wood on a wagon! Ha-ha!" I felt a definite panic as Mr. Washofsky guffawed; he enjoyed himself, but his various monitors were getting busy. I took a step toward him, but he continued to observe: "A Reform one, eh? They're sending me a Reform rabbi. Oy, I need a prayer or two, even from the Reform."

I was totally charmed by this Polish man. His crusty good nature was disarming, and I felt something warm inside drawing me to his face which seemed now a touch more possessed of color.

"Yes, Reform." I could also tease. I wanted to hear Mr. Washofsky let me have it about being of the liberal religious bent. Instead, he put his head back on the pillow, shut his eyes momentarily, and let out a breath:

"Oh, what's the difference? *What's the difference?* Does God really care? I accept your Sabbath greetings, young man. Excuse me, Mr. Student Rabbi. So *nu*, what do you have to say? Nice of you to be here. My son is in California, older than you, I think. A pretty good job he got himself, with a company which sells brochures or something to car dealerships. Something like that, what do I know? I had three heart attacks already. My wife is home now, she just left here. What's your name, Mr. Student Rabbi?"

I told him. He asked me where I was from. I said, "Right here, actually. Cincinnati."

"What are you talking? Nobody is from Cincinnati. Nobody is from America, either. You know what I'm talking? Come on: Where is your father from?"

"My father was from Israel, Mr. Washofsky. Actually, you're right. I am not from Cincinnati either. I was born in Israel also."

"Israel? That's something. I keep telling my son— did I mention he got divorced already? What can I say? What can I do? Divorced, like a bullet! I keep telling him, with the car brochures, I say, 'Take your kids, go see Israel.' That's a place. That's a beauty. I never been there."

"You have how many grandchildren, Mr. Washofsky?" I suddenly heard myself talking in an Eastern European syntax. I imagine now, as I looked for my father in Mr. Washofsky's bed, that I could not find enough ways to pay tribute to this funny old man with a fickle heart muscle.

"I have two little grandchildren. You never saw such babies. California sees them, I don't. But when I do, let me tell you. This is life for me, this tells me I'm still alive! You know what I'm talking?"

I looked at Mr. Washofsky, a Jewish man who, I later learned, had survived a fourteen-month internment at Auschwitz. I doubted that he had ever known any ambivalence about becoming a grandfather. I was certain

48

about his agony over his son's apparently early divorce. I asked him, "When are you going to see your grand-children again?"

"Actually, soon." The old man lit up with excite-ment. "He's bringing them soon, he says, the salesman. He comes with them every time I have a heart attack! Ha-ha!" Mr. Washofsky let out a cough and the flimsy bedframe shook. "Take it easy!" I pleaded, grabbing his narrow wrists. "You must remember your strength. You should preserve yourself for your grandchildren."

Mr. Washofsky looked me straight in the eye.

"Where did you read that line, in a rabbi book?"

He is a fond recollection—the dear heart patient I used to visit in the months after my father died. Mr. Washofsky remains for me as a bright light of hope and common sense at a time of confusion and doubt. His admonishment about a pat line is forever a part of my personal manual. But more important, he stands out as an example of effective ancestry at a time when I was sure that no man ever welcomes the privilege and re-sponsibility of growing ripe with grandchildren. Mr. Washofsky, whose deep eyes flashed with humor, and whose forehead formed stripes of wisdom, came along just in time. Lying in the same hospital ward where my own father was treated, the old man from Poland made me realize that my father was just a man, not a mold. Finding comfort at the bedside of the brochure sales-man's dad, I gained enough insight to forgive my father his fears.

*   *   *

The Bible hints at the possibility of identifying with a grandparent in case there is a gap where the parents should be. In the 1980s, as our grandparents continued to live longer, and as more and more fathers and mothers split up, I heard a great deal about "skipping generations." Grandparents even sought legal means of gaining access to their grandchildren; in the era of latch-key kids and full-time day care, it was not hard to understand the yearnings of some older folks to pull their lonely descendants close. A video store, a carpool, a drop-off activity at the Y do not add up to the impact of one embrace from a parent or grandparent who really knows and who really cares. If a parent failed to deliver, a grandparent could indeed give a child hope.

There was a significant level of tension in the household of Isaac and his wife, Rebecca. Genesis tells us, point-blank, about these two and their twin sons: "Isaac favored Esau because he had a taste for game; but Rebekah favored Jacob." The father preferred the ruddy Esau because this one was "a skillful hunter"; the mother was drawn to the cerebral Jacob, who "was a mild man who stayed in camp."

In a plot concocted with his mother, Jacob eventually seized the birthright which the father had intended to give to the more athletic Esau. The Bible gives strong indications that there was potential for violence between the two offspring: "When the words of her older son Esau were reported to Rebekah, she sent for her younger son Jacob and said to him, 'Your brother Esau is consoling himself by planning to kill you. . . . Flee at once. . . .' " Jacob would now be physically and emotionally estranged from his father. He did flee, and at night he trembled and prayed to God for consolation.

It is during such a nocturnal session of prayer that Jacob's true feelings of origin are made evident by the Bible. Jacob "came upon a certain place and stopped there for the night"—it was the middle of the desert, but it was more so the landscape of the boy's soul. Jacob fell asleep, and dreamed of a stairway that extended from the earth to the sky. Angels went up and down the stairway. Here, in even the most remote spot in the world, in the dark of the night, was another breakthrough, a shaft of meaning. Jacob would awaken feeling certain that God had said to him, "I will not leave you."

But I am intrigued by the way in which God "introduces" himself to Jacob during this dream sequence. After describing the divine staircase, the text reads, "And the Lord was standing beside him and he said, 'I am the Lord, the God of your father Abraham and the God of Isaac. . . .' "

The God of your father Abraham? Abraham was not Jacob's father. He was Jacob's *grandfather*. Isaac was the boy's father. Is the book confused, or perhaps just telling the truth? What happens when a youngster cannot relate to a parent, or, as in this case, when there is a complete breakdown between son and father? I have seen it over and over again—in the great, homogeneous suburbs of America.

Flanked by self-serve gasoline pumps and strip

malls, these "places" have little more geographic integrity than the ambiguous "place" of Jacob's nighttime yearning. A teenager cries out, but cannot relate to parents who are overworked, overextended, overwhelmed. Sometimes the children get no answer. If they are lucky, a grandparent emerges, carrying the wisdom of an old neighborhood where "place" still meant something. The grandparent becomes the parent. The Bible expresses this, and the biblical tradition freely encourages it: If you cannot relate to your parent, then relate in this way to a grandparent, or even to a grandparent substitute.

The biblical text does not write Isaac out of the picture; the deity is still identified as "the God of Isaac." But, significantly, this phrase comes after the encouragement to the troubled teenager, Jacob: "I am the God of your father Abraham." Parenting is not the unique possession of those who happen to be biological parents. It's an ancient truth, but it comes to play very dramatically in the 1990s, when virtually half of America's kids are living in broken homes. Mr. Washofsky, connected by tubes to life-sustaining oxygen, was nevertheless breathing life into some youngster, one generation removed, out in the remote developments of Southern California.

Every person ages differently. But the issue of people feeling connected to each other is as constant as the advancing face of our national landscape. My more senior colleagues in the American rabbinate led congregations that represented distinct communities; families still clustered together in urban habitats that had transferred from something called the old country. More veteran rabbis, in fact, still address constituents as though there were still this tribal karma built into the synagogue structure. But, like America in general, the Jews, successful, curious, ambitious, materialistic, have left Grandmother's coordinates in favor of new, gleaming, monolithic mini-diasporas along the outer edges of cities now stretched into metroplexes. My older colleagues meet at conventions and seminars, reminiscing about the old days when the president of the congregation was the jeweler around the corner. The president may still be the jeweler or the realtor or the CEO. But you're most likely to find him or her at the other side of some cross-country freeway.

This is not all necessarily a bad development, and no rabbi would really decry the right of American Jews to broaden their involvement into the greater texture of our culture and civilization. Moreover, the Jews have always been migratory; history has even proven the expediency of not always being all together in one place. (The Talmud actually justifies the dispersal of the Jews from ancient Palestine as an effective way of preventing harm from coming to all the Jews at once.) But what I find noteworthy is that many of the people I have met cling to at least the perception of, or the nostalgia for, an old neighborhood.

My congregants Lewis and Richard, Abe's sons, recall that their father and his friends came from a street in Cleveland called Kinsman Road. I hear this name constantly; the children of parents who have died say the name as though it satisfies some restlessness of their own. My own peers do not drive down this street now. Kinsman Road is the inner-city extension of blight and trouble and neglect. But many of my members who have, thankfully, lived to ripe ages will describe glorious days of community and fellowship and commerce in a now ethereal, remembered world of pretty parks near downtown, nearby synagogues, concert halls, labor societies, and local cemeteries. A Jew would walk out the door into a living community where he prayed, walked with his children, ate herring, put money into a blue tin box to plant trees in Israel, opened a business, and where he was eventually buried.

I certainly can understand and I genuinely honor such recollections; what is intriguing is the romantic association with it all on the part of second and third generations who have only heard about it. Raised now on the lawns of neat and tidy townships that are virtually indistinguishable from each other, visiting friends who have relocated to other states but who live along the edges of the same yellow arches and green interstate signs—no wonder the longing for something which they never actually had. In Long Island, I met people who had lived in Bay Shore or Patchogue or Huntington for over twenty years. Yet introducing themselves they would say to me, "We just came out from Brooklyn." In Toronto, people never really left the sublime smells of Kensington Market; in Cleveland, they dream of Kinsman and 105th Street; in Detroit's distant suburbs, they still long for the dark onion rolls from beyond Ten Mile Road; in greater New York, hurtling along the Hutchinson River Parkway, they still remember walking to school in the Bronx, in Manhattan. Their children form worship and study societies on the Upper West Side, with such modern Orthodox spasms betraying, I think, the need for at least the spiritual equivalent of the old neighborhood.

My own generation may have been caught in an emotional trap: This emergent group of post-1960s, new entrepreneurs and high-mortgage landowners is not necessarily inspired by loyalty to a location. Our parents came from urban pockets; we raise children now in places where once only gentiles lived, or where tomatoes used to be planted. This is not a negative condition, but it does give way to a yearning for heritage, and it does explain something to the regional rabbi. I find a certain nervousness, an indelible loneliness in the suburban body language of my congregants, whose civilization is increasingly controlled by automatic garage-door openers, commuter connections, and private security systems. I go out into their sunny backyards after their bar mitzvahs and anniversary parties: The air is filled with mesquite and grilled salmon, the plates are filled with low-fat pastas, the Chablis wines flow. But you don't feel that you are actually somewhere in particular. Often, it is the grandparent or the older aunt or uncle who comes into such a gathering, and, by his or her very presence, or even by a still detectable accent, gives some sense of lineage to this get-together. Even imported from a condominium in Florida or Arizona, these ancestors form the historical anchor as an extended family celebrates in the backyard tents or the catering halls of the new Babylon.

Glued to our cellular car phones, scattered further and further away from the coordinates of legendary neighborhoods, decimated by divorce figures, what will we tell the little ones who follow us? That we didn't want to be grandparents? That we never really knew the second cousin or the godparent they ask about because he or she lived in Oregon and we lived in Pennsylvania? Can a video recording of somebody's baby naming really satisfy the genealogical curiosity of a youngster more than a good conversation about who was there and why and where he or she came from? Digital equipment is useful, and the great suburban subdivisions of our country certainly provide people with fine comforts and with much-deserved relief. The synagogues and storefronts we left behind have fallen into not-so-hospitable decay.

And yet the legacy must be carried forward, across the commuter tracks, jogging paths, and carpool patterns of the post-tribal community. My departed congregant, the kind usher Abe, may have experienced some temporary ambivalence about his sons' having children. But he and his family prevailed nevertheless; Lewis and Richard reaffirmed this as they sat and shed tears with me that morning in my study. Sitting with them, I suddenly recalled my Mr. Washofsky, and the morning he admonished me about Yiddish.

Yiddish is more than a language. It is part of the oral tradition of Jewish continuity. The sound of the hybrid dialect sends even the most secular Jew into quiet fits of memory and association. The language is enjoying a modest revival in the ethnic-sensitive late twentieth century. Mr. Washofsky asked me one day: "So, do you take any Yiddish in that rabbi school of yours?"

"Yes, as a matter of fact, they offer Yiddish now at the college—"

"But do you take it, Mr. Student Rabbi?"

I had to confess that I did not, at the time. But it was not that I was not interested in the language; indeed, I was and remain possessed of a fascination with Yiddish, and would like to be able to read Sholom Aleichem's stories about Tevye the milkman in the original. But Mr. Washofsky—whom Mr. Sholom Aleichem would have probably parodied back in Poland—was still focusing on the major issue.

"But you say they have it, even in your Reform school?" Mr. Washofsky had a unique way of putting things.

"Oh, yes! Definitely. In fact, Yiddish is coming back strong, Mr. Washofsky."

I had hit my friend with one of those unfortunate pat lines again. He trembled in the rickety bed, tubes contorting, his skinny arms beginning to wave. His right finger poking into the gray air of the hospital room, he bellowed: "But dat's the point! Dat's the point! Yiddish is coming back? *It didn't go no place!* All you got to do is read it, study it, remember it, and it don't need to make some comeback, because *it didn't go no place!* Only the people—they went someplace, and forgot."

CHAPTER FOUR

"Your Children Are
Your Bricks"

Meanwhile, where is Florence, the widow of the usher, Abe, on the morning his children gather to remember and to reflect?

At one point in the session, as Lewis and Richard recall their father's special enjoyment of automobile trips in the countryside, the younger brother remarks, "If my mother were here, she would tell you." Having been through a heavy trial already on Abe's role as a grandparent, I hesitate to push the sons now on just why Florence has not come. But Richard's comment about his mother dangles in the air, and no one jumps in to clarify or complete the thought. So I ask about the mother, and Lewis responds, "She just couldn't come. She's in her own world, she just could not have said much."

That may be so, and it is basically not my business to decide who comprises a eulogy session. But I regret their not bringing their mother; her presence might have given the two daughters-in-law, Janis and Leah, more of an opening to participate. In general, I think, the women in this situation could be spared such over-zealous protection.

That men will make emotionally important decisions for women is as modern a phenomenon as the stalled Equal Rights Amendment and as ancient a problem as biblical literature. I have noticed in my rabbinate that while men dispatch women to discuss the arrangements for a bar mitzvah reception or a wedding party, they seem to have few qualms about doing all the talking when it comes to the heavier moments. I hear the pattern clearly in the story of Sarah, Abraham's wife, as she lurked behind the flaps of her desert tent.

In Genesis, Abraham also keeps his wife out of a discussion—this one being the matter of her bearing a child. This is in spite of the fact that the couple clearly wanted a child together (Abraham had offspring by an Egyptian, Hagar, but would eventually abandon the woman in the desert). The longing for their own child clearly continued for Abraham and Sarah, even as they grew considerably older. Finally, the text indicates, God tells Abraham: "I will bless her; indeed, I will give you a son by her."

But Abraham does not feel compelled to share this bit of information with his wife. One can scoff at this whole story, but it is possible, particularly in this era of home and drugstore pregnancy tests, for the man to know before the woman that she is carrying. The gentleman is more likely to hear from a lab technician than he is from the deity, but the issue of disclosure is still the same.

But that Abraham learns that Sarah will somehow be blessed, and that he does not tell her, is proven in the text just a short time later. On a very hot day, the desert wind sending the sun's rays to pound upon the sands, Abraham is sitting by his tent. Genesis reports that Abraham sees three mysterious men coming across the horizon; in fact, it's God, appearing in the form of three wayfarers. It may be a mirage, but Abraham offers the men hospitality and shelter nevertheless. They have news for him: Sarah will finally have a child. Where is Sarah? they inquire. In the tent, they are told. So be it. Nobody invites her out. But she overhears the conversation from inside the tent, and, we are told, "Sarah laughed to herself." She clearly had not been told of this before, and she does not allow herself to believe it now. "Now that I am withered, am I to have enjoyment—with my husband so old?"

Sarah was cynical, perhaps even bitter. She puts herself down, indicating little faith in her old and barren body. It is hard to read the story and not sense her loneliness. There does not seem to be a great pattern of communication between husband and wife at this stage of their long relationship. The biblical text surely indicates that women are sometimes isolated, living in a world of men.

You can hear Sarah's muffled laughter still, as the twentieth century closes. The tent flaps have been replaced by the heavy-duty bolts of suburban doorways; the sands have been paved over with driveway asphalt.

But for the most part, men still decide things together, and women find out later. This timeless human tendency has been mitigated somewhat by the feminist trends of this generation; I suspect, however, that double-income ambitions and other economic realities have been more responsible for the emergence of women than the intervention of so-called sensitive men. I see only a small cross section of American civilization, but what I see is familiar: Women wait; women serve; women react; women rebound when men are stricken by their crises. Truly, we have an entire new circle of women attorneys, women physicians, women directors, women clergy. The point is that these people are not simply attorneys, physicians, directors, and clergy. They remain the female repositories of what men (and many women still) assume are male roles.

Does the Bible have an ax to grind in disclosing Sarah's private burst of cynicism? Not particularly; the Bible is routinely telling us stories about people keeping secrets from each other. The biblical writers are the stenographers of 1990 as much as they are the recorders of the past. Indeed, the biblical text is unremitting in its pro-male bias; it even has God siding with the men in the context of Sarah's much-deserved laugh.

In the very next passage, God asks Abraham: "Why did Sarah laugh . . . ? . . . Is anything too wondrous for the Lord?" One wonders: Can't the woman account for her outburst herself? Does the man have to explain even that? But the woman is allowed only to be defensive: "Sarah lied, saying, 'I did not laugh,' for she was frightened. But he replied, 'You did laugh.' "

Is this all unfair to Sarah? I think yes; the people of the Bible are true-to-life, and I can therefore relate to their troubles and even their biases. Is the biblical text sexist? Absolutely. It has as many sexist references as this morning's newspaper. And yet it has as profound an understanding of a woman's pain as any piece of literature in human history. The references to Sarah and her love of her son, Isaac, could only have been written by a woman, or by a very sensitive man indeed.

The son born to this matriarch was named Isaac, which, ironically, means "laughter." The Bible allows for the full throttle of the mother's joy and relief as she celebrates the arrival of her child: "God has brought me laughter; everyone who hears will laugh with me." Later, the mother will endure the near death of the boy as Abraham takes his teenaged son up on a mountain to bind and sacrifice the child to God. The biblical story is that God wants to test Abraham's faith, but the mother's suffering silence in this is not addressed, nor is Sarah even consulted in the matter. The account has troubled readers for centuries; it is the dramatic and harrowing portion of Torah heard in Reform synagogues every Rosh Hashanah morning.

No wonder the tremendous amount of rabbinic commentary about the death of Sarah, at the biblical age of 127 years. The Bible states that "these were the years of the lives of Sarah." In the Hebrew text, the word for "life" is actually written in the plural. Why Sarah's *lives*? Because, the rabbinic tradition asserts, Sarah had two lives: one life before having a son, the second life with her son. Judaism has a sensitivity to the pathos of the womb; only a woman can ultimately understand the implication of Sarah's lives. Meanwhile, I got a glimpse of this when my Aunt Anne buried her son Terry.

Anne is really my wife's aunt, but in our large midwestern family of Polish and Russian descent, it doesn't really matter. The lines are blurred as little cousins have grown into graduations and weddings; nobody keeps track of such hyphenated relationships as we return to the flat cemetery in Columbus, Ohio, time and again. However, I used to appear with Cathy at such family milestones as just a son-in-law or nephew. Now I arrive wanting to grieve but am often expected to officiate in some capacity; Cathy's family presses against me, counting on my rabbinic status to lend some format.

There is another rabbi in the family, a gentleman older than me, a renowned scholar and teacher. He and I find each other at such occasions; it is mutually comforting, and a matter of great pride. The happy times are easy, and the two of us feel noble and special. The tragedies offer different challenges, but we feel a privileged cooperation in helping to manage the family's fresh sorrow. But when Terry died, I was useless in my own grief, and, like everybody else, turned to my older colleague and to the local rabbi for some solace.

Terry and his brother, Jeffrey, had buried their father just four months earlier. Uncle Elliott succumbed to a variety of ailments; diabetes and poor blood clotting had finally squeezed out the funny man who told long stories and enjoyed chopped liver. Uncle Elliott's death hurt, but it was not unexpected. Aunt Anne went to the cemetery surrounded by sons, daughters-in-law, and grandchildren. Over the soggy earth, we all wished El-liott had had more discipline; we knew we would have wound up burying somebody else if he had.

Terry did not say much about the whole thing. It was only in his general reticence that he and I differed. Like me, Terry was in his thirties, the father of little girls, a physically large man. Terry loved his full-sized van. He parked it in the driveway, or angled it in his garage with the attention of a car buff. Terry was at-taching a set of runners to the big van when the vehicle collapsed upon him, there in his garage at home. He was working underneath when the jack broke. I re-member thinking, when Cathy's father called us to tell of this ghastly event: Did God happen to be looking away?

Terry was putting the side runners on his van be-cause he wanted to make it easier for his mother to step up into the car. Now it was his mother who found him, lifeless and crushed. The ambulance arrived, but it was too late. Terry's wife screamed into the phone, sum-moning a tow truck to come and remove the van from their garage and from their midst forever.

We all gathered for the memorial service at Terry's house just after burying him in the cemetery. It is cus-tomary to say prayers in a house of mourning even after a funeral service and the committal to the ground. The room was filled with sweating men, facing eastward against the wall. Grieving in a sterile suburb in Colum-bus, Ohio, we drew comfort from the invisible pull of far-off Jerusalem.

It was so hot; human steam rose in prayer. Broken gasps of throttled Hebrew bounced against Terry's trophies and his widow's many etchings. Silent, dirty footprints filled the narrow hallway and the crowded den; we tracked in mud and tears from the cemetery. The prayers were hoarse whispers. The throats of the men were dry and raw.

Terry's children sat dazed in the corner. They were like old, drawn spirits now trapped in youthful bodies. Their presence brought a further edge to us as we prayed eastward; perhaps God could bring some sense into this house. Terry's mother, catatonic, stared at a clock which now seemed to be turning counterclockwise. In that room, the normal flow of time had been upended, and Aunt Anne's womb had been betrayed. And we prayed: *"Thou keepest faith with those who sleep in the dust. From thy hand, O King, comes death as well as life."*

The day had begun with a plain wooden box: a familiar accessory for me, but today a dreadfully personal intrusion. Epstein's Funeral Home is a barely noticeable diversion along the typically midwestern spread of Columbus's Main Street. A pale building without fanfare, it blends unceremoniously into the long boulevard of doughnut signs, fried chicken banners, and the white castles of hamburger empires. People like me try to create requiem solemnity in places like Epstein's; we eulogize, we invoke God's name, then we get into a parade of waxed cars and drive along the wrapper-strewn avenues of the test-market culture.

But today I did not have to be afflicted by such ambiguities. My cousin was dead. The funeral director at Epstein's had advised me and the other pallbearers not to use the handles of Terry's wooden box. He was a bulky man, and we had to carry his coffin by holding its bottom.

We pallbearers sat in the very first row. We were mostly strangers to each other, drawn from the various categories of Terry's brief life. But now we sat in sympathetic guard to the grief of his mother, and we were bonded by a brief and unwelcome intimacy with eternity.

A folded flag sat on the rim of the casket; the bold stars and stripes were as righteous bands of color against the plain box. Such an irony: Terry had been careful in Vietnam, but had forgotten in his garage.

The first utterance of the service came not from the congregational rabbi. From off to the left, behind tall blinds, came the muffled sounds of the immediate family. Terry's youngest girl opened with a wail: it was the language of a child left alone. The pallbearer next to me, a veteran of combat, grabbed my wrist. In me, every instinct I knew as a young father turned out from my heart and pounded in my ears. I caught a glimpse of Anne's face, hanging behind the tall blinds: She was pale; her features looked forlorn.

My wife and I arrived at the cemetery before the procession. Spared here of officiating responsibilities, I wanted the quiet comfort Cathy and I can give to one another. Now we stood alone at the cemetery. A canopy hung over velvet chairs and the fresh grave. I thought:

The earth has opened for me a thousand times; I am a clergyman, and I am trained to regard the split ground with impersonal equanimity.

But today the soil looked familiar, and I was forced to stare and be afraid. There was an intermittent rain, as though the eyes of God had finally opened in sympathy.

They came, the dismal parade of a broken generation. The sky hung low, the earth moaning in anguish. I remembered that my tradition says: "Your children are your bricks." In Hebrew, the two words, children and bricks, are homonyms, indicating the building process that comes through the generations. In the cold rain of a Columbus graveyard, however, one encountered the broken house of Anne, the mother and grandmother.

Terry's little children stepped out of the long black car. My wife's lips twisted; I saw this and knew, that instant, that no man has ultimate access to a mother's soul. The little girls walked toward Cathy. Instead of the chatter of the playground, they would soon hear the guttural despair of Aramaic lamentations.

The young widow emerged from the car. Her eyes had disappeared behind a stained curtain of salty water. Her face, normally smooth, had gone to clay. The mother came out, all but bloodless. Anne's eyes registered a cold familiarity with this field.

Graveside. We bitter men endowed with the great honor of pallbearers laid the box down upon the burial straps. I felt Terry's weight. He was like me: heavy-shouldered, direct, dependent upon the support of friends. I let go of the box last. The earth swallowed my tears, not without defiance. There was no rabbinic armor to flash.

We stepped back. The young widow sat leaning across her daughters. Terry's mother had turned to stone. As though trying to heal the gap that the ground now boasted, the women physically interlocked: It was one meshed flesh of unrelenting horror. I have seen it so often: Children begin to wipe away the tears of grown-ups, daughters stroke the hair of their mothers, nobody really knows whose water has fallen onto whose own hands.

The crowd dispersed in hurried agony. Terry's brother, now without a sibling, took hold of the shovel that lay across the heap. He thrust a mound of earth into the hole. And again. And again. A man of great dignity, Terry's brother handled the shovel like a cannon. I said: "Jeff, that's enough. You have done enough." His anger pressed against me, and he left the field with a soft, primal cry that has changed me forever.

We returned to the house where Terry lived and where he had so unexpectedly died. His widow and his children now regarded familiar things with fear and pain. We all arrived and formed a circle of absolute silence. It was the speech of the grave. We prayed the memorial service in the warm room where Terry's trophies might as well have broken, like stones in the soul.

When Cathy and I finally got home, we reached for our daughters. All day, parents and grandparents had been reaching so. A broken generation: A certain safety in which we trusted had been cruelly disturbed. Terry was like me. He and his brother and I were once three big men at the family circles. Our children have teased each other about their daddies. Our wives are still young, and, until now, had watched only their mothers arrive widowed at a cemetery.

CHAPTER FIVE

His Child, My Instincts

L EWIS AND RICHARD and their wives have left my office. I make myself a note to call their mother, the widowed Florence, some time before Abe's funeral service this day at 3:00 P.M. It is still early morning on a Sunday. The building is starting to fill with the chatter of incoming Sunday school teachers and the early children. Our Hebrew teachers are virtually all of Israeli descent; their animated conversation and social habits around the coffeepot outside my study remind me of a busy corner at the main bus depot in Tel Aviv.

I sit and scribble notes for Abe's eulogy. The sun is full outside; I have a long day ahead, with three funerals and a number of other responsibilities that will carry me into the early evening.

There is a brief knock at my half-open door. A gentleman whom I know marginally in the congregation appears. "Rabbi, do you have a minute?"

70

I look up and see distress in the man's face.

"It's about my son," he says. "I know you don't know him. He lives in Seattle. Can I talk to you? I am in a quandary."

His son? The man's son is surely *my* age. My position often neutralizes otherwise given assumptions about years and wisdom. Can I offer any advice to an older parent about life and pain? I have no choice. The gentleman is standing in my doorway; the Jewish people have invested me with the warrant.

"Sit down," I say, sliding Abe's developing eulogy under some other papers. "Sit down and talk to me."

The man's son has a drug problem. The father is not completely certain of his son's address in Seattle; the son has become an indigent. "I keep sending him money, always to different places out there. I'm not sure what's going on. He's got a girlfriend. I'd like him to get married, but I don't really know if she's helping him, or if she's into the drugs too."

What is the son using? I inquire. Cocaine, probably, and maybe other stuff. I realize what the situation is: The father has effectively, if unwittingly, funded both the addiction to cocaine and an apparent repugnance for gainful employment. The father is hurting as he gropes for the courage to cut off his own son.

"Is that what you're asking me?" I probe. "Do you want me to tell you that you should stop the money so your son will maybe be forced to pull himself together?" As I suggest this to my congregant, I wish to myself that the problem could be so simple.

But it's never simple, and the issues of addiction and

its effects have permeated the modern rabbinate like the acid rain of our new environment. I do not recall one serious seminar on the matter in my years of rabbinical school, although the Jewish community in general has come around to a sobering acceptance of this new and harrowing agenda.

Twice a week at the noon hour, a fleet of shining, luxurious sedans and hatchbacks fills up the circular front driveway of Tifereth Israel. From out of the Nissan 300s and the Acura Legends emerges a group of sleekly dressed, successful young suburban aristocrats. I pass them often on my way out for lunch. They are well-endowed, smooth, and stricken. They are the elegant drunks and addicts of the new frontier, and their chapter of Alcoholics Anonymous fills a smoky, urgent meeting room in our building.

They are not all members of the synagogue, and they represent various denominations. They are, however, overwhelmingly white and rich. They own and operate the nouveau restaurants, insurance agencies, and car dealerships of my community; I see them in various contexts around town. They have so much, and they often have little to offer. I sometimes resent the manner in which they fling their expensive vehicles, replete with cellular telephone hook-ups and vanity plates, about our lot. They are oblivious to fire zones and handicapped parking spots; they walk into the building clicking heels and tightening clothing around narrow bodies. There is surely a strong social element to this noontime gathering, but these people are sick and in need of the mutual support they offer one another. I have occasionally been a guest at their soulful communions, and I am aware that many of them have fought significant battles against strong physical obsessions.

My sanctimony about them is surely unfair; I can't help thinking of the waves upon waves of trapped Americans whose addictions are the product more of circumstance and less of indulgence. Babies born already hooked can hardly be blamed for their predicament. Poverty—a mainstream condition of our country —is ripe territory for the afflictions of crack and angel dust. America is a land of searing ironies. While I was walking once with a good colleague of mine in the manic streets of New York City, my friend observed: "What other city has both a Fifth Avenue and an Eighth Avenue?" It may be a wry observation, but we do live in metropolises whose parallel avenues reveal both shining glass and broken glass.

My congregant's son was lost in Seattle, but the story is really in everybody's backyard. I have heard it and seen it in settings as diverse as the American culture. In Portsmouth, Ohio, in 1977, it appeared to me in the form of a packed pistol.

I was a student rabbi to a congregation of twenty-five families in this somewhat squalid river town along the Ohio during the last two years of my graduate-level training. The student rabbi program of the Hebrew Union College is a particularly useful aspect of one's preparation for this work: Small towns all across America have pockets of Jewish life where old and otherwise abandoned houses of worship are serviced by students who appear every other weekend. The rabbi-to-be gets practical field experience, while these Jews on the fringes get the well-meaning if raw input of a fledgling professional rabbi. In my time, I served such outposts in Welch, West Virginia; Jasper, Alabama; and, finally, in Portsmouth.

The temple building, just two city blocks up from the riverbank and across the waters from West Virginia, was small and well kept. On a good night, forty to fifty people would come to hear me conduct a formal Sabbath service, deliver a sermon, and bless the children. The music of the service came from an old organ, played elegantly by a kind and cheery gentile woman who had grown up in these coal hills. Mrs. Knost knew the Union Prayer Book backwards and forwards and at the time had already forgotten more about Jewish hymnal music than I had ever known. Mrs. Knost and I were unusual but compatible partners, working in behalf of Jewish liturgy, there in the Scioto forests of southeastern Ohio.

A strange lad, maybe seventeen years old, had been appearing at Friday night services. His name was Billy. He told me he had come in search of the real messiah. The quest, whispered to me one evening at the post-service reception, made me nervous. I basically attributed his lonely appearances to the Bible Belt personality of this region; it should have made me even more anxious than it did to have a pale-looking, jumpy, unfamiliar boy keep showing up at these services looking for the true Jesus.

Nobody in the congregation knew anything about Billy. Knowing his rather un-Jewish background did not prevent them from still feeling grateful for an additional young participant in this Friday night ritual. Mrs. Knost had reservations, however. "I've seen him around," she said as we walked into the dark parking lot of the little temple one night. "I don't think he's a good boy. He hangs around the street corners downtown. He looks strange, like he's on something."

Billy may have indeed appeared different, but I was under no illusion that strange things were happening only to people *outside* this congregation in Portsmouth, Ohio. Its membership, however small, was certainly not immune to grievous and bizarre behavior. In my years of association with the group (I would stay in touch for some time after my graduation), there would be a murder-suicide involving an aged couple in whose home I ate a number of meals and whose grandchildren I had taught. There was also a suicide, of a ten-year-old boy whom I loved dearly, and whose family traveled to Cincinnati one year earlier to witness my ordination as a rabbi.

So it was not at all Billy's Christian faith that worried me, but the way in which he manifested a singular hunt for messianic clarification. Billy called me one night as I slumbered restlessly in Portsmouth's Ramada Inn. "Can you meet me, Rabbi?"

"No, Billy, it's too late. What, what do you want to ask me?"

"If Jesus was a Jew, how come all Christians don't go to a Jewish synagogue? And if he died, aren't we all supposed to sacrifice something too?"

I didn't know what to do with this boy on the other end of my phone line. I thought about the Methodist church around the corner, where I had given a guest sermon a few weeks earlier. What was the name of that minister? I couldn't remember. Maybe Billy could go talk to him; he was a very friendly pastor, and had welcomed me and the scattering of my congregants who had come to the annual pulpit exchange. I asked Billy if he knew the church.

"What? I never would go in there! They're the problem!" Billy was agitated, and I felt a pinch of anxiety. Would the front desk downstairs release my room number?

Billy was breathing hard on the line. His words were slurred. I saw his face in my mind, and imagined him talking to me at the temple receptions. I had never realized in person what now was absolutely evident to me, as Billy's stream of conversation poured into my sterile hotel room: Billy was drugged; Billy was "on something." Mrs. Knost's warning filled my ears.

"Look, Billy," I said, "I'm not sure I can give you the answers you are looking for—"

"Then who will?" He sounded muffled, twisted.

"Do you have a family? Do you—did you ever go to a church somewhere, maybe get to know a minister? I mean, you have some very important questions which deserve answering."

"Was Jesus a Jew?"

"Yes, Billy. Apparently, he was Jewish. And he had much to teach to a lot of people."

"Was Jesus a Jew?" It was the fundamental query of a troubled soul.

"Yes!" I was nervous now and, frankly, annoyed.

76

"Yes. Jesus, the historical person, was a Jew. Why are you asking this?"

"If he was Jewish then, and you admit it, why aren't we all Jewish, and why doesn't everybody come to hear you talk in your temple?"

I paused and raced through options. I wanted off the phone. I wanted to give this boy some kind of answer, but I also wanted to be relieved of him.

"Billy, where are you? Are you at home? Is there somebody there with you? Do you have parents?"

"I'm here by myself. But I'm going to make some friends soon."

Thank goodness, I thought. Maybe he's been diverted to talk about more mundane things.

"In fact, I'm enlisting soon. Going into the army."

"Billy, that's great. But, Billy, I think you are drinking something, or maybe you've taken something. You don't sound like yourself. If you want to go into the army, you're going to have to take care of yourself, too."

It was then I realized that the line had been dead for a few seconds already. Billy had hung up. I fell into a poor sleep. I kept seeing Billy's pale, sad face.

He was there, in the little temple, two Friday nights later. He came in just after the service had begun. Mrs. Knost looked over at me from behind the organ, even while she played. I was very uncomfortable about his being there. Cathy had joined me for this particular weekend in Portsmouth, and I felt very relieved at her company as the wiry lad sat down in the back row.

After the service, as we dispersed into the lot, Billy approached us. He seemed all right, although he stood mostly in shadows. I could smell the river nearby as I took Cathy's hand. Billy said: "Rabbi, can you give me a lift?"

"How did you get here, Billy?"

"I, uh, took a cab down." His words were, again, slurred. "Used up all my money. I just need a ride home. It's just a couple of blocks from the Ramada."

Cathy's eyes did not register disapproval, so I invited him into the rented car. He sat in back. I watched him in the rearview mirror. As we set out, I saw that he looked extremely depressed. I noted that he did not smell of alcohol, but his presence betrayed some kind of affliction.

He spoke to us from behind: "Well, I'm joining the service this week. Got the papers already."

I felt a flood of relief; I had been unable to draw a bead on this fellow, and his planned enlistment offered a solution. If he was an addict, there was little I could actually do. He offered no clues to his background or home situation. He refused to let me refer him to another clergyman, someone who might have been familiar with family care possibilities in the area. He was not my congregant. And I was very young.

Then Billy said, "I got a gun here. It's loaded. Carry it around now."

I resisted the immediate impulse to slam on the brakes. Something told me to continue driving, so as to prevent this obviously dangerous and troubled individual from becoming excited. Cathy glanced at me, keeping her cool, wordlessly agreeing with my strategy. But I did say, speaking to the rearview mirror, "Billy, why do you have the gun here? What did you bring it to the temple for? I thought you found the temple to be a peaceful place."

"I may need it. Sometimes I feel very . . . by myself. And, you know, because I already told you, I can't figure out what to do about Jesus being a Jew. You know that."

I remembered the phone conversation from two weeks before. Billy had said: "And if he died, aren't we all supposed to sacrifice something too?"

I recalled that Billy had hung up the phone on me in midsentence the night he'd said that. So now I asked him: "Billy, I'm concerned about you. Are you taking something? Are you hooked on something? Can I get you some help?"

The response came quickly: "Stop here! Stop! I'm getting out. Thank you, but I'm getting out!"

I complied eagerly. Billy stepped out. I took a glance at his face as he departed. He was the most dejected youth I had ever seen. He walked away from the car as Cathy and I—exhaling sighs of released tension—made mental notes of the location.

At the Ramada Inn I called the Portsmouth police and reported Billy, whose last name I had never learned. I gave the street corner where he had exited our rental car. I stated my credentials and my concerns about the unhappy lad.

Three days later, Mrs. Knost called me in Cincinnati. She thought I would want to know: Billy had been arrested later that Friday night, a half block from the Portsmouth Ramada Inn. He was charged with carrying an unregistered firearm and the possession of several

Quaaludes. I would never see Billy again, but I have confronted this drug and others since, now that they have acquired designer status.

More recently I looked at a picture of two young performers. The photograph sat on the counter in the dressing room of the actress whom I was visiting at New York's Winter Garden Theater. In the photo, she was standing with her friend, the co-star. He radiated sunny health, she smiled with soft prettiness.

Now the snapshot was but a flash of memory. The young man was gone, his life a powdery wisp of snowy intoxication. Big dreams snuffed out by nervous habits: I stood with the actress as she stared at the photograph. The indifferent traffic of Broadway roared outside the window.

The young man's demise was a matter of his own choosing. "He had a tendency to perspire a lot," recalled Laurie, the actress. "We knew something was not quite right."

The two had been linked by friendship and inter-relating roles in the megahit *Cats*. Laurie had already lost other colleagues to AIDS; now Kevin—a burly actor with serious prospects in the theater—had poisoned himself with cocaine.

I recalled an occasion when I had phoned Laurie at the theater. She had a long break in between scenes, time enough even to converse with a long-distance friend. We were chatting when she said, "Hold a minute—"

I heard Laurie say to somebody: "Okay, go on. Feel better. . . . Yeah, see you tomorrow, if you're back."

Back on the line with me, Laurie explained: "Kevin's going home again. He's not feeling well."

I am sure that Laurie knew very well at the time what Kevin's problem really was. For myself, I was incredulous that somebody could leave a big musical while a performance was still continuing. "We have understudies and swings," the actress told me, accounting for a perfectly normal routine in the theater. And, in fact, the cast of *Cats* had already become somewhat accustomed to accommodating the prevailing sickness of one its major players. Death came, its finality filling up the dressing-room counter of my friend. Kevin had already been replaced permanently in the show, and, since he'd always been hidden behind the elaborate costume called for in the part, the audience was hardly affected.

But in real life, people are not replaceable, and the death toll from drugs and alcoholism is as absolute as the people who have vanished. While rabbis and social workers and dependency therapists can actually do little to stem the tide of drugs that infiltrate this civilization, we can raise certain issues of responsibility. And one responsibility we have is to strenuously define drugs as killers, and drug-takers as slaughterers of the soul.

This would seem as obvious as Laurie's grief for her colleague, Kevin, or my congregant's agony over his lost son in Seattle. But people in my line of work are dealing with a dangerous and subtle tension in the psyche of today's culture. "Miami Vice," a program that confused cocaine with glamorous clothing, was a touchstone of the 1980s; baseball and football heroes, who remain the stuff of little people's fantasies, indulged in substance abuse, were slapped on gold-plated wrists, and then continued to endorse mitts and dandruff shampoos on television. But the most ominous distortion that has developed in recent times is the one between the two poles called life and death. This is why I became particularly worked up, in 1988, about the prospect of a postage stamp honoring Elvis Presley.

I was able to publish my concern about this proposed stamp in a syndicated article that originally appeared in *The New York Times*. I allowed that only because Elvis Presley is dead does he qualify for commemoration on a stamp. Beyond that, one wonders about the appropriateness. Elvis Presley died ignominiously and self-abusively, because of his consumption of alcohol and drugs. I thought that we should collectively shudder at the thought of a youngster closing a letter to a friend, then posting it with the picture of a public figure who disintegrated in a manner that can be described only as anathema to what we want kids to believe and practice.

Elvis Presley, though an American institution, became as sick in spirit as he was sublime in song. His music may have been good; his life-style was certainly bad. Elvis ended it all in a burst of indulgence and irresponsibility, undoubtedly succumbing to the extreme pressures of his signal career and the easy availability of anything he craved. But Elvis was not martyred, he was stoned.

Teenagers and young adults come to me and reveal heavy peer pressures in the matter of partying and drug taking. They feel it can't hurt them, that they won't really die. I want them to be frightened of the way Elvis Presley expired; instead the American culture allows for, and even encourages, a kind of national séance with Elvis. "Sightings" of the phoenix-king are regularly reported from sundry hamburger joints, radio stations, and mini-malls. But it's not funny: Young people, so impressionable, so heavily bombarded in our country by intense video messages, can easily become confused. If Elvis lives, or if Elvis can be re-created by greasy impersonators, then maybe he is really not dead. The message this sends to the young specifically, and to the ignorant in general, is that death is not necessarily final and that fatal practices do not necessarily cause a penalty.

This dangerous blurring of real life-and-death situations is abetted in our electronic culture by the daytime soap operas and prime-time melodramas. Characters are killed, or they die amidst much fanfare, and then they reappear in miraculous second comings. Kids watch, kids who are under pressure in corner schoolhouses to say no to drugs, and they get the message that death is not necessarily irrevocable. And then, the ramifications of this pop-resurrection syndrome leave much damage control to stricken parents, siblings, and professionals involved in social work.

As a rabbi, what do I tell the younger brother of a teenager who was killed by a drunk driver, the child of a parent who was poisoned by cocaine? I need at least to have the absolutes clear before guiding him to the therapy of grief.

If there is one thing that Judaism teaches me about life, it is that death is final. A cultural tendency toward the qualification of this ultimate truth is harmful psychologically, and it even invites reckless behavior. Every clergyman, every social worker, every schoolteacher in America is dealing with the growing national epidemic of adolescent suicide. We haven't got a chance at getting youngsters to reject suicide as an option if, in fact, it is tinged with a certain impunity, and perhaps glamor. Meanwhile, for me, having counseled so many beautiful young people in the matter of drugs, and having had to endure the burials of some who did not hear, the intake of a chemical substance is nothing less than a suicidal act.

My congregant whose son has a drug problem looks up at me. His somewhat wrinkled face is drawn with worry and isolation. His boy in Seattle might as well be hiding away on the moon. Clearly, the father is struggling for the guts to deny his son any more money, since the funds are clearly being squandered for a terrible habit. I repeat my question to the heavy-hearted gentleman: "So, is that what you are asking me? Do you want me to tell you to stop the money?"

"I guess I do, Rabbi." Again, a middle-aged man is weeping in my office.

"Then I'm not telling you something you haven't already decided in your heart. Don't consume yourself. You'll never stop sending love. But your money is apparently hurting more than helping."

The man gets up to leave.

"Wait," I say. "Wait. Listen, I'm just going by my instincts, too. You know this is a real risk. It's impossible to tell from here how serious the addiction is." I think, with deep melancholy, of Billy, of Kevin the actor, of others I know. "Look, I'll call you later with the names of some agencies out there. But you must realize, this is a serious move. You could lose your boy altogether."

"I already have anyway," says the father.

"Tell God What the Prayerbook Cannot"

I N MANY WAYS, there is no such thing as group prayer. People come together in a church or a synagogue or a mosque to worship, but ultimately prayer is a private matter. We need a liturgy as surely as language needs grammar. But the potential for prayer rests in the collective struggle of individuals, whether seated in some elaborate tabernacle or walking alone in a wood. The father whose son is addicted, the son whose father has died, the mother whose daughter is unhappy in love, the child whose parent is unemployed, the sister whose brother is captured by a cult—though encouraged by the company we give to each other in a house of worship, each of us is quite solitary in the situation of the soul.

Standing now before about two hundred youngsters—the middle grades of the synagogue's religious school—I appeal to them to sing and pray with me.

These are suburban kids with jaded edges who are not always responsive. They are not easy to convince; a living human being addressing them is not necessarily going to break through. It is hard to be impressed with their attention span; they are used to fast and bold imagery flashing before them across some kind of solid-state screen. They are, generally, bright but unchallenged, with cerebral impulses magnetically deferred to some calculator or PC unit. I feel for them: The cliché has been run into the ground, but this group, born in the later 1970s and the 1980s, really does endure a dearth of living heroes. They were born *after* the deaths of Bobby Kennedy and Dr. King and after Apollo 11 and after the clearinghouse years of Vietnam and Watergate. They are not particularly driven or annoyed by any national passions; civil rights and Indochina and even the Beatles amount to ancient history for these children of Pac-Man and the grandfatherly president who smiled at them and validated their prevailing interest in themselves.

I truly endorse the relative peace these youngsters know, and am relieved that so far they are not being pulled by some undeclared war in some far-off place. Yet I feel a gnawing sense that something is missing for them in the category of emotion. For these kids, suffering is having to walk to the video store.

I spoke to a class of graduating seniors at Cleveland Heights High School in the spring of 1989. Cleveland Heights is a transitional community of both fine estates and less regal middle-income housing, bridging the city itself and the eastern outburst of advancing exurbia. The community is an interesting amalgam of coffeehouses, secondhand record stores, and old churches. Orthodox Jews and black Baptists pass each other on streets lined with Torah academies, gray synagogues, Polish bakeries, monument shops, five-and-ten-cent stores, and a single kosher-Chinese restaurant.

The high school is, not surprisingly, a churning, sometimes even dangerous microcosm of the American urban hodgepodge. It is, however, a handsome edifice, and I found in this senior class a group of thoughtful youngsters who had a few questions about their future. They were white, black, Jewish, gentile, and all interested in what a rabbi does. I had been invited through the efforts of one of the students, a daughter of one of the more active families in our congregation. The students greeted me politely and sheepishly; I was nearly overcome when I realized that not one of them had been born yet in 1970.

"What do you look forward to when you graduate this year?" I asked.

One young man, blondish and slight, answered me, "Getting off on my own, getting away from parents telling me what to do, being free."

I thought it was a normal enough yearning for an eighteen-year-old boy—not too different from what my own high school graduating classmates had felt in 1970. But I challenged him nonetheless, because now it occurred to me just how long ago 1970 was, and how being a rabbi to kids in the 1990s requires a realigned vision of the landscape.

"When I was finishing high school, nineteen years ago," I said, "we all wanted to be free too. But we had some pressures that I'm honestly glad you don't have. And we had a little more on our minds than just what college to go to, or where to go to work. We were a little preoccupied with something called dying."

A post-MTV stupor had been broken in the pleasant classroom; the seniors wanted to know what I meant.

"You see," I began to spout off self-righteously, "there was this war in Vietnam. You have heard about Vietnam? It was a little more serious than the shows you may watch, like 'Tour of Duty' and 'China Beach.' " The students were intrigued, and I began to realize that I was a thirty-six-year-old parental model giving a bona fide history lesson. This was unsettling, but it drove home a sense of mission and responsibility.

"You see," I told them, "when I was your age, we were thinking about this war, and five hundred American kids like you were being killed every week. That's what we were seeing on television all the time, in the Vietnam War. I had two classmates—they were just like you now—who went over there and died."

"When I was your age?" Was this me talking? When did this happen? Not that I considered myself that morning to be ridden with antiquity. But, suddenly, I had a strong feeling about the process of aging. We are not young for always; already my generation and its angst have filled out footnotes in history. Meanwhile, I was standing in front of a generation once-removed from my own. If I muse about the older group's associations

with Kinsman Road, these young innocents could already smile knowingly at my inability to exit Penny Lane.

Then one of them raised his hand. "Did you go to Vietnam?"

The question was fair and timely. (I much preferred it to the previous inquiry: "Do you have a wife? Are rabbis allowed to have sex?") I answered about the war: "No, although Vietnam came to everybody who was male and about your age in the 1960s." I explained about the draft lottery system that had existed by 1970. "When I say 'lottery' to you now, you probably think of Super Lotto or some such drawing. But to us back then, it was a potential matter of life and death, of patriotism and some real guilt. My birthday was drawn in the lottery, and I just missed being drafted. Frankly, I'll spend all my life knowing that, especially since two of my classmates came back in body bags."

Rabbis often rely on stories about death and dying in order to ensure the attention of an audience, and I was plainly guilty of doing so at this moment. However, the recollection, and the desire to impress a certain urgency on this group, were genuine. Young people seem moved when, for example, they are asked to pray privately and to consider the tillage of their individual gardens. No prayerbook, regardless of how effectively composed, can speak for the most intimate and heartfelt of impulses. It was in such a moment, in the setting of my own high school, that I first realized my desire to become a rabbi.

Woodward High School in Cincinnati during the

1960s was, like Cleveland Heights High School now, a tense cross section of the urban microcosm of American society. It became an opportunity for social awareness for a handful who, like me, had matriculated to this churning pot of 3,600 youngsters from a tiny Hebrew academy. One of the most significant transitions I have ever made was from Yavneh Day School junior congregation president to assistant drum major in the Woodward High School marching band.

Although I was destined to become a rabbi, my high school years were nevertheless centered around the winning tradition of the Woodward Bulldogs football team. We were P.H.S.L. champs year after year. The Public High School League games were windblown, weekend-night, autumn affairs played under athletic field lights and the supervision of local police. There was trouble sometimes, on and by the field. Our players, our cheerleaders, and those of us in the band had to all rush back to the protection of waiting buses after victories at certain less-than-hospitable schools. Rocks were occasionally thrown at us by frustrated Withrow Tigers; some Aiken Falcons splattered our blue and white band uniforms with eggs.

Some of my former high school chums remember these years with an undeniable residue of racist feelings; they do not recall Woodward fondly. Abetted perhaps by my tolerant profession, I gloss over the incidents in my memories of those very full days and nights. In the 1960s, we were the thrown-together adolescent coalition of blacks, whites, Jews, gentiles, midwesterners, Appalachians, poor, fraternity brats, and independents who found common cause in the pep spirit of the intrepid multicultural sports clubs of our school. I remember Eddie Shuttlesworth's huge black hands grasping the pigskin snapped to him by Andy Glas, a bulky Jewish boy who made the all-league squad in our senior year, 1970. Eddie Shuttlesworth, who wore the crown of Homecoming King tilted dangerously on his enormous head, also played center on the Bulldogs basketball team. When he wasn't carrying the football, or leaping for an intimidating rebound, Eddie's fleshy fingers somehow handled a trombone valve in our motley marching band.

Like the nighttime cold that suddenly grabbed at our feet those heady nights, excitement tugged at those of us who formed the crowds in Woodward's championship seasons. My tall, skinny friend Clifton Fleetwood was the first drum major. Boarding the bus one jubilant night, Clifton pelted me with Afro-Sheen, declaring effervescently, "This is my culture, man!" In that bus, under cover of exhaust-filled shadows, we sang, dared, rocked, bellowed; the only colors that mattered flew about in the form of our majorettes' blue and white sparkles.

It made some sense in the late 1960s, and it was the product of a communal willingness at least to explore the national equivalent of Joseph's multicolored coat. It alerted me to the rabbinic injunction for social action. It gave me a pubescent insight to the rabbinic admonition: "Pray for the welfare of your country." Woodward's fight songs still ring in my ears, especially as I walk down the halls today of a place like Cleveland Heights High School.

Granted, it was not a perfect little world. From day to day, there were dangerous brawls in our school, and there were outbreaks of violence serious enough to bring paddy wagons into Woodward's front circle. More than once, the front glass windows were shattered at the G. C. Murphy Company, our five-and-ten hangout at Swifton Shopping Center across the way. Some of the things that happened to me and others in my high school do not fall into the category of nostalgia. I did not enjoy being beaten up by black bullies more than once just because I was white and appeared vulnerable. In spite of it, however, the sense of being in a kind of social laboratory won out over the troubles that came with it. It was during these years that I adopted the old rabbinic proverb "Life is with people."

I truly believe that, from time to time, a group of youngsters actually became color-blind; *being together*— around a Bunsen burner, on the raw tiles of a locker room and shower, in the crowded hallways of a Friday morning pep rally, at a lunchroom strike protesting lousy food—precipitated some level of mutuality and tolerance. Spending time now in community schools, searching the eyes of my religious-school pupils, I find it hard to realize the idealistic élan which turned many of us into clergy, social workers, teachers, general practitioners, and conscientious objectors.

I keep looking around now for a girl named Debby Siegel. She graduated with me and has disappeared, on

quixotic wings, into the post-sixties world of divorce
and avarice. Debby thrived on the atmosphere of that
school. Relatively short, with a wide mouth virtually
always in a smile, Debby walked the halls of Woodward
with a certain good-natured innocence that defied any
hostility or anger the walls of our school sometimes
betrayed. Long, frizzy, dark hair that seemed airborne,
an oval face with forgiving eyes that declared absolute
faith in humankind—I often teased this power-packed
little figure that she was "the world's first hippie."
She was not; she was, however, a nearly utopian free
spirit who personified what we, in our best moments,
genuinely hoped for in that time and place. The approaching Kent State gunfire of 1970 would qualify
Debby's good faith. Two years earlier she and I held
hands and wept when we heard, early in the morning
of June 6, 1968, that Robert F. Kennedy had died during
the night.

People like me were drawn to Debby. It was not
romantic tension that affected our relationship and that
sparked the admiration of so many boys. She was so
very bright, so able to learn from what was happening
in the school and, by implication, in our country. In that
sense, she taught the boys, with charming intelligence
and high spirits, much more about the definition of a
woman than some of our more leggy, more obviously
sexy female classmates. I cannot remember the names
of any of the majorettes on our rocking bus; I cannot
forget the dovelike persona of Debby Siegel, who
danced in Woodward's annual *Showcase* musical, cap-

tained the cheerleaders, claimed academic honors, and blue-penciled my social commentaries in the school newspaper. I look for her in today's more somber school halls, and I can still hear her greeting me. "Peace!" she said to me, time and again, in that hoarse voice which never quite gave out.

"Peace," we all said to each other quietly during the annual student walk to publicize our concern for the environment on Earth Day. We shouted it through the halls after Lyndon Johnson's announced bombing halt of North Vietnam, when the exhilaration spilled over into a spontaneous after-school Freedom March across Reading Road to Swifton Shopping Center. Mixed colors, strong feelings: Debby's expression shone when our football team defeated the all-white, suburban Princeton High School, and it sank from the fearful sense of setback and unraveling that permeated our hallways and grounds the morning after Dr. Martin Luther King, Jr., lay dead on a Memphis balcony.

That morning—April 5, 1968—was a private day of infamy for virtually all of us in that churning public high school. But I mark it as my first day of training for the rabbinate. We came to school frightened. The long circular driveway in front of the building, where we normally frolicked with milk shakes or chili dogs from G. C. Murphy's, was now a frontier of danger and tension. When I arrived that morning, some of the students were already pouring *out* of the school. Some of their faces were familiar; most of them were angry. One nasty fellow, his black face contorted with resentment, recognized me. "Kamin, you whitey Jews ought to clear out of here. You all killed Dr. King. We're going to break up the stores in Swifton."

Meanwhile, some four hundred black students filed out and poured onto the front green. They were still; they carried stunned countenances. With great relief, I recognized my friend Clifton Fleetwood in the multitude who were walking out of the school.

"Clifton!" I ran toward him, and was then stopped by the cold, even menacing stares of his compatriots.

Clifton's eyes gave me no encouragement. As he brushed by, he said, in a quivering voice: "No, man. This is not for you."

What ensued was a morning-long, quiet sit-in and vigil by Clifton and his brothers and sisters. The school shut down; some of us fled home. As city patrol cars began to accumulate about the school, another group of us teenagers formed in a corner of Woodward's front quadrangle. We remained within view of the sit-in participants, but were now culturally removed from them and their pain. (I can attest from my community work that this separation continues to this day.)

Meanwhile, the crackle of police walkie-talkies blew in the air between the two assemblies. Our group was white, mostly Jewish, and, I think, admirably motivated. For the first time, I found myself in the informal role of rabbi: As I spoke aloud for friendship and prayed silently for the welfare of my country, I was shaken inside by the vacuum in Clifton's eyes. What I felt could not be found in any prayerbook. The Jewish sensibility about this category of prayer struck me that day and has remained paramount. I discovered the outer layer of my soul on that April morning, and that layer is indelibly American. It is a good coating, serving well the deeper elements of my essential Jewishness.

Now, I look at this assembly of my religious school students, and ask them to pray silently. "Tell God whatever a prayerbook cannot. . . . Pray for peace. . . . If there is someone you know who is sick, if there is trouble for you at home . . ."

There is true silence. A soft refrain is then begun by the guitarist. I wonder what kind of world they will inherit, these gatekeepers of the next century. Certainly, prejudice will graduate with them from school into the increasingly neat, racially antiseptic suburban developments of Middle America. They will pump gas at self-serve booths and will sigh at the apparent proliferation of cancer in an era of high-level medical technology. It is not improbable that somebody out of any group of contemporary kids will die of AIDS.

Looking into their eyes, I ask myself: Just what does scare or delight the youngsters of the 1990s. *Can* they pray privately? What a challenge to be a rabbi today! My peers dreamed dreams, and we had to rely still upon our imaginations. Today, they process such things on videotape. Who was really better off?

CHAPTER SEVEN

Pressing Against a Child's Pain

I

T IS now nearing 10:00 in the morning, which would mark the end of the Sunday worship and assembly with the middle grades of the school. With a few moments left, I ask the assembly if anyone has any particular concerns or comments. Many issues have been addressed over the years in this weekly gathering of students, teachers, some parents, and rabbis: We have annually lit six large candles in remembrance of the six million Jews of the Holocaust; we have arrived in costumes for the holiday celebration of Purim; we have enacted dramas recalling the liberation of the Hebrews from Egypt; we have collected and boxed canned goods and sacks of rice for our adopted hunger station in Cleveland. One very unhappy Sunday morning, we spontaneously remembered and consolidated our grief over the seven astronauts of *Challenger*, who had perished in the skies that same week.

"Who has something to say or ask?"

A hand goes up near the rear of the hall, attached to one of the older boys—a lad I know for both his intelligence and his ironic insights.

"Rabbi," says the young man. "I have something I'd like to show you and everybody."

"And what would that be, Todd?"

"It's a certificate," the boy answers, trying to conceal a wry look on his face. But he is giving himself away. The adolescent fuzz on his face, the little wrinkles around his mouth, the rather dark eyebrows are forming in conspiracy.

"What kind of certificate, Todd?" I know I am headed for interesting (if not rough) waters.

A pause. Todd draws upon his innate sense of timing. He knows I will not get upset with him; he's too bright and contributes too much that is ultimately useful. But this was a particularly big moment for this likable if sometimes irreverent teenager who loves to challenge his teachers.

"Well, Rabbi, I guess I'm your colleague now." Whispers are breaking out in the assembly, and Todd is capitalizing upon his moments in the sun magnificently. "Let me show you."

The young man walks down to the front of the hall where I am standing. Without hesitation, he stands next to me at the microphone. Emphasizing his movements, he pulls out his billfold and produces a folded document. Sighing with forced solemnity, he unfolds the paper and presents it to me: It is a license from an alleged seminary in the Southwest, and it certifies that the bearer is now an ordained clergyman, Mr. Todd Green-berg. Reverend Greenberg, speaking carefully into the open microphone, announces with aplomb: "It cost me five dollars."

Laughter breaks out in the crowd.

I say, genuinely shocked: "Five dollars?"

"Plus postage, Rabbi."

I manage to settle the school down in the aftermath of the little pastor's startling revelation. Todd, adventurous, calculating, agile, has made himself a good point, particularly in the context of the televangelic culture he sees and hears. I demand of my religious school pupils that they understand Judaism's basic revulsion for such gratuitous religious claims. The profession of clergy has suffered yet another little disgrace on this morning of the five-dollar diploma.

You can certainly send away for almost anything in America, including skin conditioners, radar detectors, and massage therapists. Todd's clever presentation notwithstanding, I regret that divinity is among these commodities, and that it has become, to some extent, commercialized and traumatized to the point of a silly joke. Television rabbis are uncommon, but that does not necessarily offset the poor image of religious professionals being exacerbated by the clergy of churches of the solid state.

You can find virtually all you want on American television, including, regrettably, liturgics and homiletics. It is clear to me in my work that faith is an intensely intimate affair. Televised religion goes against the grain of this. What should be a private concern is instead mixed into the same cable-converter-box frenzy as "Wheel of Fortune" and Andy Griffith reruns. Neither Vanna White nor the amicable sheriff of Mayberry do any harm. I just would prefer to leave my prayers stored in my heart and not in a VCR-augmented Nielsen meter.

It is not for me or any rabbi to be judgmental about any of the well-known television preachers whose dramatic fund-raising appeals or personal misadventures made news in recent times. But it is for me to clarify with my congregants, especially young, impressionable congregants: Jim Bakker and Oral Roberts are not my professional colleagues. They are businessmen whose product is segmented prayer and whose method of conveyance has more to do with Arbitron patterns than with knowing their "congregants" personally. We have already conceded the suburban experience in America to a series of golden arches and divided highways. Must we also franchise human prayer?

When youngsters ask me about being a rabbi, I tell them that it is a noble profession. I trust that Todd Greenberg and others like him—whether they consider the rabbinate or not—will know this and believe it. You have the chance, on any given day, to bring a sense of healing to a family in grief, to a kid in trouble, to a sick person suffering the little indignities of convalescence. You are called upon to speak in favor of human dignity, on behalf of neighborhood peace, on the side of a drug-free society.

All these opportunities are as real as the integrity of your spirit. It is hard to imagine that kind of commitment truly conveyed or received across a video monitor. I am sorry that so many Americans apparently relegate the matter of their spirituality to some ecclesiastic talk-show host. Television has its powerful place in society, but it cannot claim to be the repository of what is holy. In real life, rabbis, ministers, and priests work in private worlds. It is safe to say that most of us have a fairly upbeat view of human nature, and that we are optimists who enjoy the moments of life's cycles. I regret that a group of self-serving television actors have come along to diminish the job description which I very much treasure.

The irony is that we are there when people need to rebound from the trouble that television boldly presents to the public. A chilling example of this occurred in the aftermath of the explosion of the *Challenger* on January 28, 1986.

It was in this same auditorium of Tifereth Israel religious school, during the Sunday assembly, that my students expressed themselves after the tragedy. We brought in the little ones, from kindergarten on up through the middle grades. Many of these youngsters, in a variety of secular schools, had been watching television screens the previous Tuesday at the noon hour. Afterwards, in one household after another, parents and children had been talking, sharing, emoting, sifting through the predicament: The effect of the *Challenger* explosion left us grown-ups with an unrelenting feeling of weakness because the violation occurred while the kids sat watching television in their seats. Now, in our temple, more than a handful of parents drifted into the auditorium where they knew the children would be praying. *"Your children are your bricks. . . ."*

The kindergarteners, including my own Sari, knew who the "space teacher" was. Sari was, with her class, lunching on sandwiches and milk in the Lomond School when the shuttle disintegrated. With the now-indelible image—a strangely Big Bird–like spread of white smoke against a benign blue sky—technology had turned a macabre vision back to my daughter's teacher and her charges.

I spoke to the gathering of children: "All week long, I saw something beautiful even as you dealt with a great sadness. We all looked to each other as we tried to deal with the pain and the fear. I heard you ask each other: 'Did you see it when it happened?' We drew very close to each other. Now we need to hold hands, to share our sense of connection. Sometimes a whole nation, people of all different colors and religions, needs to be a family."

The little ones had a powerful need to speak, in between our hymns and prayers. First-graders stood up and described their confusion: "I didn't understand why they couldn't fly away from the smoke." "Where are they now?" "At least they're in the sky, so God won't have trouble finding them and taking care of them." The students ruminated about mountains on Venus, about saluting dolphins in the Atlantic Ocean, and about the seven days of Creation.

An older child brought to our attention that the Soviet Union had, in fact, named two peaks after the two vanished woman astronauts aboard the *Challenger*, Dr. Judith Resnik and the teacher, Mrs. Christa McAuliffe. "I think that's beautiful, Rabbi," said the normally reticent lad who had been touched by this particular act. "Maybe we can realize that we are all the same."

A third-grade group had brought a mural to the service, which they fashioned in their classroom. It depicted the school of dolphins which had "saluted" the falling wreath sent to sea by the astronauts' colleagues at Cape Canaveral. Many people had been deeply affected by this widely reported act of nature; it was truly a poignant salute to the doomed attempt by seven souls to *challenge* the heavens. "But," as another youngster announced, "they were seven brave people, all different, but all working together as a team and united in a dream." A large Jewish candelabra, with its traditional seven candles, was ignited in memory of the *Challenger* crew.

We made careful note that the American national family was proportionately lost in the explosion: white pilots, black aviator, Asian-American specialist, Jew, gentile, Buddhist, scientist, schoolteacher, fathers, mother, children. We dwelt heavily on the seven distinct souls who perished, naming each one individually per candle. Like the seven days of Creation, each had its own light, purpose, characteristics.

I told the children, hoping to get through, that the untimely demise of *Challenger* brought with it a lesson: "Life can be short, it surely is precious. Children and parents should not put off saying to each other, before it might be too late, 'I love you.' "

"And now," I implored, "who has something more to say?"

A little boy, about nine years old, raised his hand hesitantly. "Yes?" I smiled at him.

"My friend's cousin was on that spaceship."

"Who was that?" I walked toward the urchin in the third row of the auditorium. Although he spoke in just a whisper, the room was in a hush, and all hung on every word.

"Judy Resnik." The reply came with solemn dignity.

It was plausible and would be confirmed: Dr. Judith Resnik had family roots in nearby Akron, and was especially remembered by Temple Israel of that community. Indeed, for American Jews, there were particular frames of reference regarding the two women who had died in the *Challenger* tragedy. Certainly, we grieved fully for the five men, and, like all of America, drew no distinctions in our sorrow. But Dr. Resnik's special connection for us was obvious: Her first name *means* "Jewess"; our pride in her life means we are proud of ourselves as Jews. When we learned (for most of us did not know) that the dark-haired scientist was also an accomplished pianist, we all sighed like Jewish mothers and fathers.

In addition, I discovered, as both parent and rabbi, the unique feeling my community had for the vanished "space teacher." Christa McAuliffe's remarkable effect on us had to do with many things. She came out of the schoolhouse; she sat with little children. When there is trouble in the schoolhouse, even the crustiest parents and neighbors come running for the children. The *Chal-*

lenger disaster was—put in the harsh language of these harsh times—a hostage-taking at the schoolhouse with no mercy. The children were trapped by the televised image; their innocence had been lifted forever. I found myself, during those dark last days of January 1986, talking about death and dying with my five-year-old Sari long before I had planned on it.

Meanwhile, I came to understand my affinity for Christa McAuliffe. My daughter's teacher began to look like her; every schoolchild seemed to belong to the space teacher. Her modesty and apparent good nature drew me to the story of her work, and I found wisdom in her simple lessons. Then I realized that even as I felt the ethnic linkage with Judith Resnik, I also felt bonded to this other young woman because, in this fateful situation, she was the rabbi.

Simply put and correctly understood, *rabbi* means "teacher." The Jews have added the historical embellishments of preacher, organizer, fund raiser, social worker. But when rabbis are working, they are educating. Whether in a classroom, in the front of a hall, in the cemetery, under the canopy, by the hospital bed— what I'm doing is teaching. Rabbinic Judaism is learning Judaism; its language is the language of knowledge and growth. Moses of the Bible, known as "our rabbi," taught; his students were the children of Israel. Having the most profound effect upon emerging human lives, it is our teachers who have led us through the generations—this is basic Jewish history.

When, around the year 70 C.E., the Romans destroyed the Holy Temple in Jerusalem, our rabbis saved us by building Torah academies. Legend has it that the Romans were delighted to supply the buildings for Jewish schools. Better the rebels should carry on dissertation about God than plan any more ambushes. The Romans are gone; the Jews are still learning. When great teachers have emerged and taken us to new places, the Jews have honored them by calling them rabbis.

Judith Resnik was the Jew; Christa McAuliffe was the rabbi. The young mother was "ordained" in the vicinity where we tend to locate God. Like Moses, she did not reach her physical goal. Like Abraham, she undertook a mission of discovery in a new and strange place, having been willing to "get out." I thought to myself, as my students lit the candelabra one bittersweet Sunday morning: No American could not be changed by the path of her brief but exciting adventure. No Jew could not have sensed her symbolic role as rabbi.

Todd Greenberg of Tifereth Israel religious school replaces his certificate to the ministry in his wallet. It is just past 10:00 now, and time for regular classes to begin. Somewhat reluctantly, I bid the youngsters good-bye, and they begin to file out. We have prayed together, thanking God for the advancing seasons, for the history of our people, and for the freedom to understand all of it. We have also prayed privately, adding unscheduled and unstructured meditations to the long liturgy of an old and historic people. The Torah scrolls in the ark behind me are round; the beginnings and the ends turn in a continuous circle.

On their way out, some of the children shake my hand, while others are sheepish. Now one fifth-grader stops by to say to me: "I prayed for my father this morning, Rabbi. He doesn't like me and my mother anymore." I read the kid's face and direct a teacher to get me his name.

CHAPTER EIGHT

"The World Is Too Much with Us"

I N MY BACKYARD, someone evidently once planted the divided shoots of a leafy flower that appears most every springtime. These peonies arrive, spreading crimson and emerald brilliance into a normally placid suburban enclave. The peonies, however, cannot appear without the intervention of a most unlikely group of necessary interlopers: our intrepid army of backyard ants.

These soldiers emerge, according to their own natural clock, to eat away at the tight outer coverings of the prenatal bulbs. Their appearance is as much an integral part of the creative process as the original burst of light which yielded the first vegetation and the primal beasts. The ants, called from their own mysterious brumal hibernation, nibble at the leaves until the mildly fragrant, elegant blossoms debut. It is not an altogether pleasant thing to watch, but it is a small solar miracle nevertheless. Cathy and I are rewarded most every spring by these floral descendants of China, unless they are caught in a late Midwestern frost.

It is easy to appreciate the delicate balance at risk in this quiet backyard cycle. If nobody steps on the anthill, or plucks the peony stalk from the soil, then the springtime spectacle will likely happen. As it says in the biblical Song of Songs,

> The blossoms have appeared in the land,
> The time of pruning has come;
> The song of the turtledove
> Is heard in our land.

This poetry is based upon the good faith that nature will not be assailed. Blossoms, like children, cannot withstand abuse. If a child is left to neglect or, God forbid, to abuse, if the ants gnaw away but do not recede in favor of growth, then all that remains are spoils.

Whenever a child pleads for attention or cries out for help, I am reluctantly reminded of a lost infant named Louis. The association is not necessarily fair—not every appeal by a youngster represents the extreme category of family violence. Nevertheless, Louis, a baby whom I never knew or even saw has left me with an unyielding feeling of the deepest grief. In this case, as in so many, a human life was snuffed out for no apparent reason save indulgence, and the earth received a body denied even its soul.

Louis's relatives were not members of the small congregation I once led in Bay Shore, New York. Bay Shore, a salty, unassuming town along the banks of the Great

South Bay, represents a foil to the traditional perception of Jewish Long Island. Fifty-five miles east of Manhattan, the village is not known for corned beef sandwiches, Hebrew bookstores, or great catering halls. Having come out of the more intense family circles of Brooklyn or Queens, the local population had assimilated long before the early 1980s, here and in nearby South Shore points such as Babylon, Islip, and Patchogue. The primary concerns in Bay Shore, one of those dots along the Long Island Rail Road, include clamming and the ferry business that services nearby Fire Island. Bay Shore supports two modest synagogues; the Jewish Center and Sinai Reform Temple are tucked away in a community whose major coordinates include Entenmann's Bakery headquarters and the South Shore Mall.

The fact that the family of the infant Louis, though not affiliated with the temple, sought me out was not so unusual. Routinely, rabbis, particularly in the greater New York area, are contacted and hired to conduct weddings, bar mitzvahs, and other occasions. Not infrequently, I found myself talking to a total stranger from Huntington or Deer Park or Farmingdale. "Rabbi, I've got the catering hall for June 23 for my daughter's wedding. Now, are you available?"

I have only a few recollections of the family situations which I entered into under such conditions, but I still maintain a calendar cycle of memory for a small child called Louis. Every spring, as the ants withdraw from the emergent peony blossoms of my backyard, I observe a private *yahrzeit* for the little baby, whose bones and

111

ashes I unwittingly came to bury one forlorn morning.
Yahrzeit means "memorial"; the one-year-old, clearly
not destined to leave footprints in this world, is inscribed in God's memory by my reciting a prayer for
him each and every blossom time.

Little Louis's death came as a result of protracted
neglect and misuse, although, during my involvement,
the case was not officially closed by the Suffolk County
Police. The baby was found alone in a welfare hotel just
a few doors away from the White Funeral Home. It was
the young funeral director, Tom, a gentleman with
whom I worked frequently, who contacted me. White
Funeral Home was nonsectarian, but immensely sensitive to the needs of both local synagogues, as it was
the *only* memorial chapel available to us in town.

"Rabbi, you've been asked for in this case."

I couldn't imagine why. News of the infant had
drifted through the village; not in my wildest dreams
had I imagined that there would be a connection with
me or my community.

"But why do you need me?" I asked, sickened to
learn from the director about the child's bruised and
lifeless body. I trusted this young man; we had been
through a number of long drives together to distant
burial grounds on eastern Long Island or, occasionally,
in New Jersey. He was not Jewish, but our similar ages
and family situations, and the common predicament of
being with people professionally at a time of grieving,
had created a bond. We were friends; something is
bound to happen when you travel together in a loaded
hearse, dressed in black suits, negotiating tollbooths or

even pulling up for a welcome repast at a diner (this would be *after* an interment).

The undertaker explained that the dead infant's only available family was a thirty-seven-year-old grandmother claiming Jewish roots. "She's the only one we have to talk to about the service for this baby," said Tom. The parents were apparently both hiding. This was part of the mystery being investigated by homicide detectives. Meanwhile, I could tell that my friend the director was not completely certain about the Jewish ancestry in this family.

I asked: "Have clergy from other faiths been asked?"

"Well, yes," came the sheepish answer.

"And—?"

"I'm embarrassed to talk about it."

"What do you mean?" Now I was a little suspicious.

"Look, what can I tell you? A couple of people were asked to do it. Let's just say *they* had no doubt it's a Jewish family."

"What? You mean, just because of a thirty-seven-year-old woman who claims to be a Jewish grandmother, they are so certain?"

"Rabbi, for whatever it's worth, the grandmother has been asking for a rabbi from the beginning. We didn't take her requests all that seriously. I certainly did not feel that this was your problem. I spoke to a minister from nearby. But the grandmother—she's the only one who even cares enough to look after all this—has insisted on a rabbi."

I was uncertain how to respond. I was appalled that the intimation of possible Jewish blood had evidently prevented any Christian clergyman from taking on the case. What if the baby were not Jewish at all? Could I truly officiate? But how could I not? How would I feel if I confronted the alleged parents, who were being implicated in some way in the death of this child? I felt such revulsion against the whole group of them: faceless, malevolent, indulgent teenagers leaving a young grandmother to tend to this pitiful situation while she made some tenuous claim to Jewishness. Where did I fit in this awful business?

I thought of my own baby, Sari—two years old at the time. She played in our backyard, near Penataquit Point in this little town by the water, not a mile from the shanty-hotel where little Louis had been left for dead. "The world is too much with us," says the rabbinic tradition. We would try to shield our children from the ills of this society, from violence and drugs and disease, but we can only shut it all out so much. What did this episode about a little infant have to do with me?

I confess to rarely feeling—as many clergy undoubtedly do—that I am compelled to act by divine will. I remember John F. Kennedy's very Jewish-sounding admonition: "God's work on earth must truly be our own." I believe deeply in, and teach about, a creative, founding God who set off the processes of life with a shaft of light. I believe just as profoundly in the human partnership needed to continue creation. Does God tell me what to do? I am not aware of any such direct inspiration, although I trust that God is there for me when I need some comfort, some gentleness in the midst of looking for the answers. I reject the evangelists because of their presumptuous claims that this or that is what God wants them to do. I have difficulty with the fundamentalists among my own people who are so certain they have all the answers that they write half the world out of providence before even completing their morning prayers.

If any religious zealots have a quarrel with me, I encourage them to read the Bible. It is a sublime book, filled with a practical, psychologically redeeming approach to the mystery of human life. It relies heavily upon human initiative, and it gives us credit for being thinking, creative beings. In Deuteronomy, near the end of the Hebrews' long trek through the desert, Moses is summarizing the possibilities for divine intervention in human situations, and tends to *downplay* the role of messianic or apocalyptic safety valves.

God's law is surely to be heeded, says the aged leader, but then Moses turns over the responsibility for follow-through: "This Instruction which I enjoin upon you this day is not too baffling for you, nor is it beyond reach. It is not in the heavens, that you should say, 'Who among us can go up to the heavens and get it for us and impart it to us, that we may observe it?' Neither is it beyond the sea, that you should say, 'Who among us can cross to the other side of the sea and get it for us and impart it to us, that we may observe it?' No, the thing is very close to you, in your mouth and in your heart, to observe it."

So I rely on my instinct a great deal of the time. If God is working with me, so be it. I cannot imagine that a loving, creating God would work against me, even as

I cannot imagine waiting around for some kind of scriptural sign that I should proceed one way or another. I shudder to think what the consequences are of such naïve, if well-meaning, inaction. I have no understanding of those who withhold relief or medical care or just plain good help to their friends or even their children while waiting for God or an agent of God to bring sanction. Self-righteousness and religion usually wreak havoc; common sense and religion make pretty reliable partners.

Still, I did come to feel, that strange morning in Long Island, that God must want me to officiate at the funeral of the baby Louis. This unusual burst of sanctimony had to be the result of all the unsettling circumstances. I relented to the plea of my friend the undertaker and accepted the responsibility.

Who would I talk to? There was no father to consult; he had disappeared some time before, emitting exhaust and other fumes from behind the wheel of a beat-up convertible. From Tom's description, I imagined that life had caved in on the cigarette-smoking, beer-guzzling fugitive, and now police looked for his pizza-splattered twin-cam Chevrolet which had served poorly as the family car. The mother, though ostensibly in shock and supposedly in town, had also suddenly vanished. Driving over to White Funeral Home, I looked for her—with no idea of her appearance—in the declining storefronts of Bay Shore's downtown strip. She remained hidden during the ordeal, trapped incognito in an adolescent marsh.

As for the young grandmother, I was not able to

speak to her either. I had been instructed by the authorities, who remained on the periphery, not to ask this woman any questions because the whole sorry thing was under investigation.

The funeral director pulled up to my home the next day in his plain black sedan. My heart was in a knot as I joined him in the car. He looked at me with eyes that betrayed that this was something new even for him. Then, to my horror, he picked up a little white box which lay on the seat between us. It was no larger than a cigar box, and it was sealed with gray tape. Not meaning to, the undertaker caused the box to shake as he picked it up to show me. Cremation is not completely consuming. Louis's bone fragments rattled inside, muffled only by his sifting ashes. I said, choking on my own breath, "Let's get the hell out of my driveway." I would not draw a comfortable breath, in fact, until hours later.

The ashes of the lost child were put into the ground without parents present and with his religious background uncertain. There, in a corner of a general cemetery which I would never again enter, I prayed that God would determine the baby's physical and spiritual heritages. Three people, none of whom could really look at me, arrived for the service. The grandmother, shockingly youthful, shapely, with bleached hair and sunken cheeks, sobbed into a pair of torn gloves. She never spoke to me; I tried to comfort her as the undertaker buried the little box, but we had too wide a gap between us.

The other two who were there included the brother of the baby's vanished mother, and a woman friend of this uncle. They said nothing and appeared eager to quit this cemetery.

If God does get news from the earth, then he certainly cried that day. The circumstances of Louis's death were speculated about in the Long Island media. Criminal charges were suggested against the proprietors of the notorious welfare hotel; this was apparently not the first time that human life had ended within its rooms. I have forgotten the particular newspaper headlines. But I do have a scorching memory of the three anonymous people, related to this forsaken baby, who came and stood with me on that sunless morning. I remember that although I said some Hebrew prayers in that field, there was a total failure to bring any reason to that scene. Louis's child-parents had failed in being mother and father. The situation was fractured, and the earth won out with indifference. Perhaps this is why I watch my backyard ants now, somewhat obsessed that they complete their task and that the peonies bloom in victory.

What do we say when a child dies of abuse and neglect? We can comment that it happens every day in America. There is not a great deal any of us can do individually to allay the ongoing national malady of family violence. However, child neglect can be apparent, and neighbors or friends or teachers can and do contact proper authorities to deal with the problem when it *is* evident. It is a delicate matter for a rabbi: If you accuse parents you risk provoking grievous feelings, but you can no more stand by and do nothing. If somebody in and around that welfare hotel in Bay Shore knew what was happening to Louis, he or she apparently lacked the integrity or courage to speak up.

In another situation in that same community, I was phoned at home very early one morning. The caller identified himself as "not one of your more active parishioners." But he needed me to come over to his store. What was the matter?

"My son has hanged himself, Rabbi."

The eighteen-year-old boy, dressed only in women's underwear, was being cut down from the noose as I arrived. The place of his suicide was, in fact, the father's lingerie outlet. I learned quickly that the parents were estranged, and that the young man apparently had difficulty emerging from the trauma of their separation. The father, still on the scene that morning, announced to me, "Randall made his choice today. Life goes on for me."

Incredulous, but controlling my anger, I inquired if the boy and the father had spoken together much. Clearly they had not; had a poor boy ever cried out louder to his father than with this rope and these panties?

Over the next few days, both before and after Randall's funeral, I also came to understand something else: Other family members and some close friends were aware of the boy's mounting agony and his apparent sexual confusion. Why didn't his parents ever hear him?

I kept these thoughts to myself. In Randall's pathetic case, it was my job to comfort and relieve and to lay his body to rest in some peace.

A wise and caring modern rabbi, the late Joachim Prinz, once spoke to an ecumenical gathering in Washington, D.C. Joining forces with his friend and colleague, Rev. Dr. Martin Luther King, Jr., Rabbi Prinz told his audience that *neighbor* is not exclusively a geographic term but a moral concept as well. It was later that day that Dr. King delivered his "I Have a Dream" message. The rabbi, who was from Newark, New Jersey, brought to Washington the wisdom of Sinai that day: Living next door to each other means that souls ought to mingle. If there is trouble next door, one must a find a way of being a neighbor.

It would seem perhaps the statement of what is obvious, but good, caring instincts on behalf of neighborhood children we *know* could go far towards alleviating potential problems. Surely this would be more useful than a shrug by the fence, or a perfunctory glance at the milk-carton photos of the missing. There is no way to prevent violence against kids altogether, or always to detect parental neglect. But there are proper interventions in tragic parent-child situations; here is where common sense and compassion work especially well with spirituality.

Children are abused in our country, sometimes even left to die. When a youngster tells me that he is praying for his father because "he doesn't like me and my mother anymore," I may very well be dealing with a marital situation or a gap in familial communication. But

I am going to try to learn as much as I can about it; the bones and ashes of a boy called Louis compel me to this forever. I am going to hope that this child's neighbors are alert without necessarily being intrusive. Cain said to God: "Am I my brother's keeper?" The answer, as the Bible tells us, came from the sound of Abel's blood, pounding from beneath the ground, against God's ears.

CHAPTER NINE

Ministering in America Lite

I T IS a little after 10:30 in the morning when the religious school administrator comes into my office. "I'm afraid I need you to go in the boys' rest room," says Alice. "Apparently, Tommy Kalb is having a problem, and, well, I can't go in there. The other boys aren't helping me, and there is no other man around right now. Would you mind?"

"Thanks, Alice."

A young couple is coming to see me shortly about their future marriage, and I'm concerned about the time. I have three funerals to conduct today, beginning in less than two hours. I think quickly about the old usher, Abe, whose sons and daughters-in-law I saw earlier in the morning. I haven't really had time yet to compose my thoughts about Abe, whose service will be at 3:00. My eulogies for Mrs. Dubnick at 12:30 and for Mr. Garvey at 1:30 are ready. There is also a wedding ceremony at 5:30. But now, it is apparently on to the boys' room to see about little Tommy Kalb.

As I begin to get up from my desk, however, the intercom on my telephone beeps. "It's Mr. Bookatz," says the student covering the office phone on this Sunday morning. Mr. Bookatz, a friend and congregant of the synagogue, is also the director of one of the local funeral agencies.

I pick up the receiver: "Yes, Barnett?"

"How are you today?" Barnett speaks to me, as always, with practiced deference. He works a lot with rabbis and enjoys their respect and cooperation. He performs a critical function for us, making our jobs perhaps a bit more manageable: He is usually the first person the newly bereaved family speaks with, and he is certainly the one with whom they make difficult arrangements such as selecting a casket and vault.

"Everything is set for your one-thirty funeral," he tells me. "You know it will be at the college chapel, not here. Our driver will take care of you. We know you're busy today."

"So aren't you handling my twelve-thirty and three o'clock services as well?"

"Yes, I am." Barnett already knows I want something.

"So aren't *you* driving to and from each of these services?"

"Yes, I am, my rabbi. Would you like me to pick you up and take care of you through the day? This will for me be only a pleasure."

"Yes, I would appreciate this very much," I say,

genuinely anticipating this nice fellow's company during the progression of three consecutive funerals. "But you don't have to come here to pick me up," I tell him. "I will drive to your place and leave my car there. I have to get to our other building later for a wedding." Working with my congregation's two sites often involves tricky logistics.

"Would you like me to arrange to have your car washed while it is parked here, Rabbi?"

"Oy," I sigh, looking out at the sunny morning. "I just had it washed."

"Okay, next time," says Mr. Bookatz. Then, applying one of his favorite phrases, which he assumes makes him sound like a person who craves Yiddish: "So, I will talk on you."

Now I walk into the rest room, where a couple of little boys are busy washing out combs in the sinks. "Oh, hi, Rabbi," says one, clearly surprised to see me. "We're just finishing up," says the other, a bit more confident. Then he continued: "What brings you here, Rabbi?"

This question catches my interest and touches a raw nerve somewhere. I truly like children, and, frankly, enjoy the ones (like Todd of the ordination certificate) who have a a little gumption. A good-natured tension between rabbi and schoolchildren has never done me any harm. This time I am unable to stop myself from saying: "What's the matter, you don't think rabbis ever go to the bowl?"

These two race out, giggling feverishly.

I wonder to myself if I should have said it, and then decide it's not worth the worry. Meanwhile, where is Tommy Kalb? "Tommy?" I ask out loud. "Are you in here?"

"Yes, Rabbi." The voice is high-pitched and fretful. Also, it comes from behind a closed stall. I say solicitously: "What's wrong, young man?"

"It's stuck. The door is stuck. It won't open, and I can't get out. I told some other boys but nobody would help me."

I walk over to the stall. "Okay, Tommy, it's okay. Let me try and open it." I pull at the door, but it really is sealed. "Wait a minute," I say. "Tommy, do you have it locked?"

To my chagrin, the kid starts to laugh from the other side. A moment ago, he was a frightened puppy. Now he mocks me.

"Of course it's locked! That's why it's stuck, Rabbi."

"All right, okay," I say, taking command. I think for a flash how amazing it is that I am involved in such a discussion. "Now, listen, Tommy: Climb under and crawl out. I'll get you as you slide through. There's room between the door and the floor."

"I can't."

"What do you mean you can't?"

"I'll get dirty from the floor."

"You what? Tommy, please. I want to get you out. You can't get out by the door, it's jammed or something."

"Rabbi, can't you pull it open?"

Just then, another boy walks by. "Hi, Rabbi. What's happening?"

I am very glad to see him. "You're Cohen, right?"

"Yes. Why, what did I do?"

"Nothing. Don't be silly. Listen, climb under here and help Tommy Kalb get out."

"No way!" It's Tommy—directing the crisis from behind the sealed stall door. My own childhood seems to be flashing by me. Then Tommy says as the Cohen boy sleekly disappears, "I'll climb out over the top."

"No, no! Don't be silly. You'll fall into the bowl. Look, Tommy, I need you to work with me here. The floor of our temple is always kept clean. Trust me, I'm your rabbi. Just slide out, and we'll see each other out here in person. What do you say?"

"Okay, okay." Doing me a major favor, Tommy Kalb makes his way out of the shut stall from underneath. Embarrassed, he stands up and looks at me with wounded pride. "Sorry, Rabbi."

"Come on, don't be silly. I mean it. Look, go on to your class. But listen, just between you and me, be sure and bring your zipper up before you leave. You've had enough trouble for one day."

As the youngster makes his way out to the free world, I make a mental note to tell the custodian about the stubborn stall. I give the door one shove, for the principle. It swings open, practically sending me through the wall.

Pulling myself together, I realize that I am standing, in a dark suit, by myself, in the boys' rest room of Tifereth Israel's suburban branch in Cleveland, Ohio.

*   *   *

I was similarly alone, in a dark suit, on another occasion: at Temple Sinai in Toronto, in 1978. A small wedding was about to take place during the quiet afternoon hours of a Sunday in summer. I had arrived early because it was to be the first such ceremony I would perform as an ordained rabbi. Walking into the round chapel of wood pews and blue tints, I saw that there were no candlesticks and no cup of wine on the table under the canopy. Somewhat alarmed, I went to seek out the temple custodian, an affable wrinkled gentleman named Wilbur, who lived in an apartment above the temple's auditorium.

Wilbur was in his fifties but looked much older. A white mane of hair covered his head; Wilbur was Scottish, and Scotch was his favored beverage. Rarely did the custodian's breath not betray his drinking habit, although he managed to get his job done. Wilbur also could not be found without a strong Canadian cigarette dangling from his lips, and he wore drooping, thick, black-framed eyeglasses. I never saw Wilbur actually light up a smoke; he was always puffing away at what I came to believe was the same continuous cigarette. Indeed, so convinced was I that Wilbur was using the same cigarette over the years that I called his brand *Ner Tamid*, the Hebrew phrase for "eternal light."

Now I needed the custodian. The wedding ceremony was scheduled to take place in an hour or so, and I was a little indignant that the setup was not complete in the chapel. Never mind that I was young and new at this, and therefore a little more high-strung than usual. I was going to march right up to Wilbur's apartment and get him activated!

Later, I would wish I hadn't. I found the narrow stairway which lurked behind the stage in Temple Sinai's auditorium. As I walked up, the lingering fumes of ash, smoke, and alcohol began to fill the air. I had not been up here before. There: Wilbur's doorway appeared to be slightly open; I thought I heard voices from within. I pulled up to the door and called to him. No answer, though I now definitely heard him and what I thought was a rather husky voice for a woman. The words were muffled, and short. I pushed the door open.

Wilbur never looked more jaunty. He lay diagonally across his cluttered coffee table, partly dressed, bouncing gleefully across the hefty figure of a woman who was not at the moment making a fashion statement. Neither party was actually stark naked; I may have arrived too soon for the full matinee. What I did behold was the back of Wilbur's white head of hair in suction between two bountiful globes of human flesh.

I did not have to clear my throat or anything. The lady saw me first, from behind Scotland. Sending poor Wilbur practically across the room, she shot up and disappeared, like a sturdy gazelle, into the deeper confines of the little flat. By now, I was scurrying back into the doorway, rushing for the steps. Wilbur was a pinwheel of eyeglass frames, ivory cowlick, incorrectly buttoned workshirt. I heard him call out to me, with stifled burr, "Did you need something, Rabbi?"

I was already a third of the way down the stairway.

I yelled up to Wilbur, trying to be casual: "Just wanted to make sure you were going to set up for the wedding in the chapel."

"Absolutely, sir. I was just now thinking of it."

Actually, Wilbur did a fine job, although I am sure he lost the girl that day. The truth is that my accidental voyeurism was but one aspect of a wedding situation which was discombobulated in a number of categories. My first official nuptial responsibility was also most unforgettable.

Sidney and Melissa, who would be married that afternoon, were not necessarily made for each other. This had been obvious to me upon our first meeting. She was tall, sightly, and completely terrified. And why not? He was muscular, attractive, and had already been married three times.

"But I married my second wife twice, Rabbi, so it really is only two times before. I keep telling Melissa this."

Melissa was not easily reassured. "Do you think we should be doing this?" she would ask me repeatedly, in Sidney's presence, in my study.

"I can only say that the question troubles me," I said, increasingly apprehensive about this curious couple.

Sidney was sanguine, however. "Pay her no mind, Rabbi. She's just nervous, like all brides."

"You would certainly know about that," chimed Melissa, gray eyes troubled and salted.

It is not for me to make a judgment about whether

an intended couple should or should not be married. We who are rabbis can neither play God on these questions nor be expected to deliver nuptials with some kind of warranty. If I have strong reservations, they can be hinted at, or I can strongly suggest some kind of premarital therapy. But nothing can be imposed; rabbis are charged to arrange "holy acts" such as marriage. Sidney and Melissa, who never acted on my strong recommendation that they seek counseling together, also never backed down on their mutual interest in a ceremony that Sunday afternoon.

"Besides," Sidney said as he took me aside on one occasion prior to the wedding, "if it doesn't work out, so we'll get a divorce."

In my first year of being a rabbi this was the most troubling thing ever said to me by a congregant. Sidney was certainly talking in the context of his own rather aberrant personal life, but his casual comment betrays a significant and disturbing tide in the undercurrent of our civilization.

"If it doesn't work out, we'll get a divorce" is not just the defensive jab of the nervous bride or groom. It is the socially accurate indicator of a new order of business promulgated by my generation of New Age amorists. When I run into former classmates of mine from Woodward High School, I am struck by how many have already passed through marriages. Now, twenty-plus years after the love festivals of the 1960s, I can barely keep track of the breakups going on in my congregation. Time and again, people come to me and murmur something to the effect that "Our parents stuck through an unhappy relationship. They stayed together, even when they were miserable. I'm not going to do this to myself."

This is a widely touted rationalization, particularly endemic to my peer group, and hard to dispute completely. It's true: I myself have come across a number of older couples who have aged together in stubborn, proportionate contempt of one another. They might have spared themselves and their families a lot of discomfort by facing facts a long time ago. But at least they went into marriage in an era when such a commitment was solemn and entered with the sense of implicit permanence. Now, it's just too easy to walk away from it, and it's not even socially regrettable. Marriage—like canned peaches, like beer, like rock music—is "lite." Living in America Lite, floating on lite cuisine, lite drinks, and lite reading, young lovers come to me to discuss their future, and, not infrequently, get "heavy" only when it comes to the prewedding legal contract. They tell me, in equity-reserve solemnity, "We have a prenuptial agreement. Our attorneys have taken care of things so that there will be no later misunderstandings."

Long gone is the trusting, spontaneous, frizzy-haired outreach of my dear Debby Siegel and her gang of free spirits. "Only love is real," sang our poet-composer Carole King, in those days before romance had been bushwhacked by litigious determinism, when attraction did not automatically require legal safeguards. Enter the rabbi, raised in the passionate playing fields of the 1960s, forced to contend with the tentative, measured love politics of a new era in which the way out is built in.

I have no right to question their careful, legalistic, and sometimes redeeming groundwork for what is 50 percent inevitable in the culture of loving lite. After all, men and women often pursue relationships in what can be described as a living equivalent of the contemporary staple—the salad bar. The dating scene, where partners pick and choose from the spread of casual contact, manifests itself in taverns, community clubs, and gymnasiums. It is increasingly difficult to bring young singles together under the auspices of the synagogue; it's too "heavy" and implies the presence of "losers" who may not even have health-club memberships. Meanwhile, busy singles keep it "lite" while working to become light. Only muscles are meant to get bulky; the strength of the human heart now seems to have more to do with pumping iron and less with producing feelings. Indeed, of all the things I find saddening today in the category of love, it is the fleeting quality of its association with burning, throbbing *emotion* that most afflicts me. I know people who speak clinically of their "good friend" or even of a "significant other," but who profess love and commitment only when it comes to oat bran. A person will break into a sweat these days for certain aerobic standards. But for a good bout of romance? Don't depend on it.

And if love does evolve into marriage, that does not necessarily mean entangling complications. You have to go back to Kinsman Road to find not only the milestone golden anniversary but also the kind of willingness to work hard at love that comes with it. Now, what used to be called going steady more aptly describes the nuptial scene. To the horror of shaken, reticent grand-parents, the divorces of their children are easily liti-gated.

Divorce—a word once not spoken in public—has fallen into the category of "no fault." Here is my lament as a rabbi: Where there is no potential fault, there is also no responsibility. If it doesn't feel good, we'll break it off. It's easy, fast, acceptable. Possessions are redistrib-uted, social patterns readjusted, sweat suits refitted, and children remanded to the tyranny of judicial carpool settlements. And why? Sometimes because two people really could not live together anymore, and will now spare their children the theater of their combat. But sometimes also because somebody did not feel like fig-uring it out anymore, and the lite culture winked across the video monitor: "Just walk away. You don't have to try."

Melissa and Sidney might have saved themselves some agony by not showing up that afternoon at the chapel of Temple Sinai in Toronto. It might have been predicted: Ten weeks later, I heard from the perpetual groom: "Rabbi, I guess I should have known. . . . You know, she went into this so uncertain, so wound up."

"Where is she now?" I asked him, hoping I would not have to endure another premarital session one day with him and a fifth bridal candidate.

"She's in hospital, Rabbi," he said, his tone reeking with concern and solicitude.

By the time I got to Branson Hospital to look for the defeated bride, her husband was already drawing on his legal people for paperwork and perhaps for protection. Melissa lay in bed, a tall, comely figure with raven hair. She had been admitted for exploratory surgery of some kind; it was not clear to me what her actual ailments might be. Melissa opened her eyes, but did not recognize me.

"It's Rabbi Kamin, Melissa." I had walked in from the sunny street.

Now Melissa, much to my relief and delight, began to chuckle. Her teeth flashed as she hoarsely declared, "Very dark glasses, indeed. Are they going to change so I can really see you?"

In fact, I wore FotoRay glasses in those days, which took time to brighten. Melissa, broken and defeated in spirit, had opened her eyes to behold a masked man peering down at her. Thankfully, I not only hadn't startled the unlucky woman, but had actually given her the path to a breath of Sarah's ancient laughter. Only now I was not laughing, as my photosensitive lenses cleared, and I saw the purplish bruises across Melissa's cheeks and under her eyes. Melissa had been beaten up; the case passed from me into the courts.

My business is the human comedy, with the term comedy understood in its classic definition. The Greeks produced great comedies, which poignantly defined life as a passionate amalgam of humor and sadness. Standing by in a dark suit, I am the Jewish referee at such ongoing dramas. The Greeks often concluded their great religious revels, the *komoidia*, with elaborate feasts; I frequently find myself at such catered affairs in the suburban corners of America, following upon a wedding, bar mitzvah, baby naming, or funeral.

Irony fills the pages of my emotional diary; my first wedding, that of the unfortunate Melissa and Sidney, turned out to be strictly unfunny. And yet it is perhaps a tribute to the unpredictable nature of this work that recalling the very first funeral I conducted brings on a smile. You just cannot be sure in this profession when you might be thrust away from the luminous interpretation of scripture in order to rescue a little boy from the bathroom stall or to lay to rest an old Jew whose family doesn't even quite know what a rabbi is.

I certainly would not have pictured myself conducting a funeral and quasi-military burial in Wabash, Indiana, during the summer of 1977. But Max Reingold, a ninety-three-year-old veteran of both the Spanish-American War and World War I, had died. Max had no wife, and no children, and had been one of the last Jews to depart this historic old village which was the first city to be illuminated by electricity. Max's family had been instrumental in setting up the display of landmark courthouse lights in Wabash; now a smattering of Max's cousins, nieces, and nephews were gathering to remember the ancient veteran.

Max had died in Los Angeles, his residence in later years. In the summer of 1977, I was a senior rabbinical student working as a program director at a Jewish summer camp outside Indianapolis. It should be noted that only an ordained rabbi licensed by the state can solemnize a marriage ceremony. Any Jew, however, can stand and officiate at the funeral of another Jew. That is why

I would be able to conduct funerals at my student pulpit in Portsmouth, Ohio, and why the task of committing Max Reingold to perpetuity fell into my unlikely and reluctant hands.

The call had come from the one community funeral home in Wabash to the rabbi of Indianapolis Hebrew Congregation, a leading liberal synagogue. Could the rabbi travel to Wabash, about seventy miles away, and officiate? The rabbi suggested that the task could be deferred to the nearby Union Camp-Institute, with its rabbi director and cadre of rabbinical students. He called the camp director, who thought it over. Here was a good opportunity for one of the clerics-to-be in this camp of living Judaism. So I was walking along in the heat of the day when Rabbi Klotz, the director, approached me. We were both in our typical camp outfits: cut-off jeans, nondescript T-shirts, baseball caps.

Rabbi Klotz said to me: "Kamin, don't you have a dark suit with you here?"

I did, but it certainly was a strange question to be asking me at 1:30 in the afternoon, in between rest hour and early free swim.

"Yeah, I've got a suit. I'm going to a friend's wedding in a couple of days." It was true: An old buddy was being married at Indianapolis Hebrew Congregation, and, although I could not officiate, I was going to say a few words. Cathy had helped me carefully package my one black suit in our luggage as we set out for camp that summer. I had no plans to disturb the outfit until my friend's wedding. Now I was quite apprehensive about what Rabbi Klotz wanted from me. "Ron," I inquired, "what do you want from my suit?"

"It's great you have it here. Great thing about the rabbinate is that a dark suit does it all. We'll take care of the dry cleaning. You're on your way to Wabash to conduct a funeral. By the way, have you ever conducted one before?"

"You might have found that out before you asked about the suit."

The next day, after having spent some orientation time with both the camp director and the rabbi in Indianapolis, and after having spoken across a static-filled connection with a second cousin of Max Reingold's in Wabash, I set out. The intrepid wedding/funeral suit felt awkward on me in the summer camp environment I was accustomed to; I had slipped into the raiment of a new, forced awareness. I actually welcomed the opportunity to go out and conduct this funeral. One actually hopes, as one prepares for this profession, to break in on such occasions under neutral, anonymous circumstances. Max Reingold's body had been returned from Los Angeles; here I came, a circuit-riding intern, to offer comfort and guidance and to learn about how it's all done.

As I walked into the ornate funeral home in Wabash, I found—much to my surprise—that the first person I would meet was none other than Max Reingold. Max lay in state, his nearly century-old body already flaky and gray from the week's travel and relocation. This was a shock to me, but I found myself nevertheless most perplexed by the fact that Max was wearing his eye-glasses, and that the lenses were distractingly crooked upon his brow. Resisting the impulse to readjust the glasses, I briskly walked past to the back halls, looking for somebody to interview.

Soon enough I was greeted by members of Max's family. Pleasantries were exchanged, and a number of comments on my youth and calling. "Are you Robby?" asked one endearing niece from nearby Fort Wayne.

"No," I replied innocently. "I'm Ben."

"I know that," she said, seemingly baffled. "But aren't you the robby?"

"Oh, the rabbi? Yes! I mean, yes, I am the rabbi here, and my name is Ben." The others in the anteroom where we had assembled looked at me gravely. I wished I hadn't brought the suit to the camp that summer. Mean-while, I had a problem: Max was lying out there, com-plete with eyewear, in an open casket. The open box not only distressed me personally, but it is against basic Jewish tradition to conduct a funeral with the deceased on display. Beyond that, the funeral home had posi-tioned the dais directly above the bier; I would be eu-logizing poor Max while he stared up at me, with corrected 20/20 vision. This was not going to work.

I began to explain to the gathering of relatives about the Jewish sensibility on closed coffins. We ought to remember the dead as they were when they were alive. I recalled to myself, as I often do, how grateful I was not to see my own father lying in his wooden box; better my recollection of a vigorous, ruddy sportsman. Beyond that, I told this group, Judaism simply pleads for the dignity of the dead, and this is facilitated by giving the dead their privacy. All this was to little avail, that warm afternoon in Wabash, Indiana. Though Jews, these Hoosiers lived in a Christian world, and they could not relate to my more intense, urban Jewish context. Said one of them about my request that the casket be closed, "That's not the way we do things around here."

I suggested that the family retire to another room and think things over. I felt adamant about closing the casket; besides, the whole scene out there, with body, box, and eyeglasses just plain upset me. Now, the funeral director, tall, throaty, Dantesque, walked in on my brooding.

"Rabbi," he said, "the family wishes to learn about your fee."

My fee? I honestly had not considered the issue. I was still the idealistic student. I said, thinking it was the right answer, "I don't have a fee. I only want to help."

"You really ought to reconsider. The family is proud, and genuinely wishes to present you with an honorarium for your service today."

I thought about it. Maybe I could take care of two issues with one bold stroke. I asked the looming director: "Have they decided what they are going to do about closing the casket?"

"Well," the gentleman sniffed, "they cannot make up their minds. Of course, we will do whatever they want, or you request."

"I'll tell you what. Tell the family that my fee is seventy-five dollars if the casket is open, and fifty dollars if the casket is closed."

The lumps on the undertaker's neck appeared to pop. "I beg your pardon?"

"That's right," I said, feeling on a roll. "Go ahead and quote my prices."

"Well, all right." He turned, like a lanky flagpole, and marched out. A moment later, I heard a sound. *SLAM!* It was metal against metal. The casket was clamped shut. Then the funeral director walked back into the anteroom, presented me with five very crisp ten-dollar bills, and showed me into the chapel.

I eulogized Max Reingold, and then, following a procession of Indiana war veterans, buried him in a fine old cemetery of grass and poplars. Taps was solemnly played by an aged bugler whose military cap teetered in the tulip-scented breeze. When I returned to my little station wagon and made my way back to camp along Indiana Highway 15, I felt a swelling of affection for an old Jew named Max Reingold.

CHAPTER TEN

"And I Am a Catholic"

THE YOUNG COUPLE who come to see me at 11:00 this morning are tan, comely, filled with dreams. He is a producer for a regional television magazine program. She is a veterinarian with a specialty in treating horses. She looks the part: willowy, equestrian, shining. Vanessa is probably more comfortable around mares than she is with me this morning; I am the rabbi she has to meet, and she is a practicing Catholic who has fallen in love with my young congregant, Greg.

Greg and I have never met, and I really do not know his family. He is nervous, even resentful. It seems to me that he has had little contact with rabbis and feels hemmed in by the requirement, apparently imposed, that he meet with me and discuss his situation. "My parents wanted me to talk with you," he says, not covering his evident reluctance to do so. "They seem to feel that I have a problem. All I know is that I love Vanessa and intend to marry her. I hope you can be involved, since my parents have a feeling for this temple, and want a rabbi present."

"Do *you* want a rabbi present?" I jumped right in.

"It would be fine, though it's not critical."

"Let's back up a bit," I say, sensing problems ahead. "I'm glad you both are here, and—no matter how I may or may not become involved in your eventual wedding—I really care about your well-being and want to be helpful."

Vanessa sits quietly, like an exotic stranger who will bide her time through this awkward situation. She seems unruffled, emotionally neutral. She lets the passion flow through her defensive fiancé, obviously knowing well that the young man's strong feelings will carry the conversation. I think to myself, wistfully, that the Catholic girl with the shimmering black hair seems more at ease with me than the Jewish boy with the bulky arms and the religious chip on his broad shoulder.

Now, in my study, I feel that I am about to sift through a kind of emotional triage.

I want him to be happy and at the same time to feel good about being with his rabbi. He arrived with anger barely in check. What is he carrying in his heart? Surely, love for this fine woman who gives him satisfaction, and whose credentials as a person and a professional are undoubtedly impeccable. Also, however, he has come into the synagogue this morning with an innate sense that I, as the agent of the Jewish people, will bear down with disapproval, with lamentation, with the burden of a thousand dark moments in Jewish history. He loves her, but he lives also with the tension of being a Jew: She is from without; she is delivered via the crosswinds of the Jewish diaspora, arriving against the tide of what even the most secular Jew knows is the unyielding, inflexible predicament of Jewish birth. We are few in number, even in golden America, and we are proportionately obsessed with the quantitative survival of our people who, numbering 18 million worldwide in 1933, have only now been replenished to 14 million in the embers of the Nazi Holocaust.

Poor Greg: I understand his agony. He loves her, and, while protesting indifference to Jewish continuity, is trapped by its pervasive hold on him nevertheless. She, meanwhile, does not have as much at stake. Her church is not necessarily in throes because she will marry a Jewish boy. The church will accommodate them both happily, and their children as well. I have occasionally wondered if the Jewish player in such a scenario does not sometimes unconsciously resent the other one's seemingly less complicated passage through; the Jews bring a threatened psyche to this crisis-filled moment, and we afflict our children with it. We raise them in the suburbs of North America, surrounding them with the embellishments of the mall culture. Our street corners are filled with choices: There are large, inviting stores to explore; multicultural schools to raise taxes for; social and business hurdles to overcome. Neighborhood churches—their cold, white statues of St. Joseph or the Virgin Mary gleaming at us in the floodlit night—pull at our deepest fears and our broadest desires to entertain their enduring mysteries. We did not move our children to Israel; we stayed here. Nor have we adopted other, more observant family rites. Our neighbors are eclectic, interesting, compelling, often worthy of our respect. Our children meet their children, and they fall in love. The predicament is America at its truest.

But while the children sing of *amore*, the parents bear pockets of pain. I see it and hear it on a regular basis; the national movement of Reform Judaism has developed a field project called Outreach for our congregations to promote understanding and mitigate suspicion of those who are directly or indirectly affected by intermarriage. It is a worthy program, but one can often best understand the issue when sitting across the room from the parent who feels threatened by it.

A fairly prominent woman in our community came to see me in the office about a public affairs radio program she hosts. Not a member of the temple, she was reluctant to discuss personal matters which nevertheless tugged at her heart. In the midst of small talk, I shared that Cathy and I were about to drive our daughter Sari to the same summer camp in Indiana where I had served years ago (and from which I had emerged to conduct that first funeral in the town of Wabash). I said to the woman: "I hope Sari loves the place as I did and that she enjoys the communal spirit of camping."

The woman's face darkened. Had I said something wrong? "My son went to that camp," she began. "It is truly a wonderful place, and, I'll tell you, he became very committed to Jewish life there. He really loved it. He felt he belonged. My husband and I felt satisfied that we got what we wanted from his going there."

The woman paused, then said: "My son became SuperJew there. Now he's twenty-one, and, as much as I felt assured back then that he would be okay, now I've got *tsuris*. Let me just say to you, Rabbi, send your kids to camp, but don't send them for a college year in Europe!"

"What do you mean?"

"He went to France on a scholarship for his third year. He was so motivated, like we hoped he would be, so sure of himself, that he earned an award in school. Went to France a Jew, and he's coming back this week holding on to a French Catholic girl he's smitten with. He loves her so much, he's thinking of becoming Catholic."

"So you haven't seen him yet, or met her?"

The woman nodded.

I offered, "So there is still a lot to talk about. You'll see what the story is."

"What use will my words be? The two of them are already wrapped in emotion. My son will express himself. We taught him to be honest. That's what the Jewish tradition tells us, doesn't it?"

I had no reply.

The mother looked at me, saying, "I am sure she's a fine, caring person. I know that matters. She certainly has good taste. She's lucky to get the boy we raised. Maybe they'll have grandchildren I can tell stories to, in case my son forgets who he is, and where he came from."

On that very same day, when a mother remembered her son's camp years and then anguished over the path of his adult life, a father came to me to recall his wife and to brood over his son.

He had phoned me first: "Rabbi, may I come to see you? I have something I need to talk with you about, better in person." Mr. Lapidus had lost his wife eight years earlier. He still carried pictures of her in his wallet, in his pockets, in his glove compartment, in his desk drawers at work, in sport coats which hung, between mothballs, in the closet at home. A dry cleaning man who is friendly with Mr. Lapidus came to the synagogue one morning to drop off a photograph of Mrs. Lapidus that had been cleaned and starched in Mr. Lapidus's dress shirt. I brought it over to Mr. Lapidus, who was slicing bagels that day at a temple breakfast. Handing over the image, I could only smile and hold back my own tears as Mr. Lapidus said, "Oh, thanks, Rabbi. God, wasn't she beautiful? They should be happy to have found it, the dry cleaners. Better a picture of my Emily than a thousand dollars found in the pocket."

What else would Mr. Lapidus say?

Now he had called, and there was concern in his voice. Marching into my study, he cleared his throat and reminded me of something I knew very well: "You know, Rabbi, I lost my Emily eight years ago. God, she was beautiful. Let me show you a picture. Now, here's the thing, I loved her so much. We raised three just plain beautiful children together. They're all grown up now. They are quality people. They are their mother. They take after me, too, it's true. But let me tell you, they all look like Emily, and they favor her, too, the way they're just— What can I say? These are quality people. Let me show you some pictures. I have all my kids here in these photographs. Oh, here: Did you ever see a picture of Emily? We had a thirty-year honeymoon.

"Anyhow, Sammy, the oldest, he's fine. Married a lovely girl, not Jewish. But they're okay. The children are being raised Jewish. And you know what? The girl is a doll—what else matters? Here's a picture.

"Lucy is the middle one. Exactly like my wife. We were all the happiest family. She's okay too, married this soldier, his uncle was Jewish, I think. They don't have a religion in the house. But they don't have children either, so what do I care? Lucy's in this picture here.

"Now, Eddie is the baby, and the one I came to talk to you about. This is a wonderful boy. He graduated high school, thank God, two months before Emily died. He's been traveling for a few years. Came home last month with a girl. She's absolutely sweet, who could not like her? If Emily hadn't been Jewish, would my heart have told me not to love her?

"Now, here's the thing," continued Mr. Lapidus. "She's a Catholic girl. She wants a church wedding. Can I blame her? But a church wedding? I mean, I can't imagine sitting there. It's a fine thing, but strange to me, to my family. They went to a priest. The priest has no problem with her marrying my son. He would just do the same ceremony as he always does, no questions asked. My son thinks I should agree to them being married in a church. I came here to get your advice."

"Well," I said, "I was about to ask you, what does Eddie think about all this? His role is key. If he's asking you for your approval of a church wedding, then obviously he is still interested in what you have to say, and he maybe needs your blessing to proceed."

"Oh yes, he's waiting for that," said Mr. Lapidus, working hard to keep his normally good spirits up.

"Look. They fell in love. You know how that felt. But I think your son has some responsibility here, to you, to the memory of his mother."

Mr. Lapidus looked up at me: "That's it. I think I feel that way. I don't want him not to have the woman he wants, but maybe, since she won't consider converting, maybe they at least can find some neutral ground to get married. Okay, so it can't be here in the temple. But it doesn't have to be in a church, either. Look, I know I can't change my son's mind, and I'm not sure I really want to. But I was wondering, and that's why I came here, what *can* I say to him, what *can* I expect from him?"

"You're right that you really cannot tell him whom to marry and whom to love. Nor do we banish our children, or even mourn them, like some very strict branches of Judaism, if they marry out of the faith. What's the point? He's your lifeline, he's the living extension of your wife. But that is exactly why he has to hear you on this, and has to be willing, I believe, to compromise on the site of this wedding. He has at least to respond to his generations. I'm afraid I think that he cannot just be allowed to walk away from his people without some settlement. And, Mr. Lapidus, I honestly believe that something is telling him this, and that is why he's waiting for you to take a position on this church wedding. For my part, though I cannot take part in such a wedding, I surely would be delighted to meet with your son and his fiancée, and to try and reassure them both that this synagogue and I care about what's happening to them."

Now Mr. Lapidus was smiling, but it was not so much in response to my speech. A twinkle in his eye, he said, "I booked their party already. I offered to pay for it. It's going to be here in this building!"

"Does your son know?"

"Oh yes, and it's fine with him. So what do you think, maybe you'll come, have something to eat, and give my son and his new wife a blessing upon the occasion of their marriage?"

"Mr. Lapidus, your son is lucky you're on his side. I would like to get to know whom I'm expected to bless. Let's get them in here, and then we'll see what develops."

"Thank you, Rabbi."

As the gentleman got up to leave, a photograph of Emily Lapidus fell from his side pocket. I am certain that another copy of the photo was in Mr. Lapidus's hand on the day, four months later, when Eddie was married by a priest at Our Mother of Sorrows Church.

But with Greg and Vanessa, there is no lightness, no sentimentality, on this Sunday morning. The television producer and the veterinarian sit before me now, an air of uneasiness slowly developing in the office. Greg does not appear to have questions; he comes equipped with answers. He begins to talk to me about something he learned years before in the temple religious school.

"Didn't Abraham break some idols?" he challenges.

"What?"

"Didn't Abraham, as a young boy, break some idols?" Greg reiterates.

"Well, that's the legend, yes," I say, a bit thrown by the young man. "What's the point, Greg?"

"The point is about conversion. Abraham was the first Jew, right? Abraham and Sarah?" Greg shot the names of the biblical couple past me in a slightly mocking tone, as if to suggest I did not necessarily know to whom he was referring.

"I think I know who you mean. Yes, our tradition indicates that Abraham and Sarah chose Judaism as adults and that they were father and mother of this people. Actually, they were the first monotheists—we give them the credit for pioneering the notion that there is one God." I glance at Vanessa, who sits in silent deference.

"The story you refer to," I then continue, "does not actually appear in the Bible. There is a fable added to the ongoing biography of Abraham that as a boy, he became upset that his father, Terah, was the town idol maker. So Abraham supposedly shattered a set of little idols in their family living room. Greg—what do you mean to say here?"

Greg, suddenly more at ease, looks at me.

"That story is not in the Bible?"

"No, sir."

"I never knew that! I've always loved that story and what it said about Abraham. All this time, it wasn't in the Bible. But it makes me think about Abraham in a certain way."

"That's the idea, that's why the rabbis added it to the pot."

There is a momentary lightness among us. They are two icons, this man and woman with strong features and ambitious thoughts. I was unsure of myself, even intimidated by their physical and emotional symmetry, as they entered the room. Now, although vexed by what Greg was pursuing via the Abraham diversion, I feel more in control. Greg seems a little vulnerable, after all, as he sits there hovering over his Roman Catholic helpmate. It makes me feel good to offer him at least a bit of rabbinic teaching; maybe I can reach into him now and offer some friendship. He seemed so cold at first.

"Greg, what fascinates you about the Abraham story?"

"I like that he rebelled when he was sure he was right about something. But it's more than that. You see, everybody wants Vanessa to convert to Judaism so this wedding can supposedly come off in the right way." The lightness is quickly vanishing. "I don't understand this about our religion. It's all so fired-up important for her to convert. But, my God, Abraham wasn't even Jewish most of his life, and he certainly managed to make an impact on the world. I remember learning that he was in his nineties before he even got circumcised. He became Jewish when he was moved to do so. Vanessa doesn't feel moved to do so now. Maybe she will later. But what she does feel is love for me. She feels this, and my people want her to change her soul before she can claim me as a husband. Isn't that wrong?"

"When you say 'my people,' who do you actually mean?" I truly want to know; it is not a leading question.

"I mean my family, my religion, everything."

"I can't comment on what your family wants from her, and if they want her to convert to something, I want to believe that it's not a matter of changing anything about her, but a question of bringing your life together into some common starting point."

"We have that already!" He is raising his voice. "We have each other."

"That is very plain to me. And I don't want to interfere with that. I did not initiate this meeting, but I do want to finish it with a sense that there was a point to your coming here. Your parents, Greg, and your family, Vanessa, owe you this: their understanding, their good wishes, and also their commitment to how they raised you both. Vanessa, what does your family say, and, if you would not mind telling me, what do you want?"

As she speaks, her eyes fill with tears; I imagine her treating an ailing pony, speaking in healing tones to the animal with soft voice and gentle insight. "I want us to be normal," she says, striking a chord in my heart. "When I met Greg, I fell in love with him immediately. It felt, and it feels, as normal for me as who I am. And I am a Catholic. That's how I was raised. My family went to church, received communion, had little parties when a new pope was elected. I didn't plan it—my life evolved this way. When I thought about the man I would marry, I did not pray for a Jewish man, a Catholic man, a television man, or any kind of man except someone who would give me love back. Maybe I was being silly, imagining that just by loving a man, everything would work out. I didn't really even think much about Greg's being Jewish until not long ago. My family? It turns out they are worried about this. I didn't even know. They love Greg because I do. They want me to be happy. They, of course, fully expect me to be married in the sacraments, in the church."

"Is this what you want?"

"I wouldn't know how to want anything else. And I certainly don't want to be made to feel guilty over it." She looks at Greg tenderly; clearly, he has been acting as a shield against what she understood to be his family's great resistance to the wedding picture she has just painted.

"What we want together, Rabbi," Greg now joins in, "is for you to be in a wedding which would also have Vanessa's priest. We have thought a great deal about this. We have tried very hard to talk it through, away from our parents, away from the tensions that always come up, especially when my parents are around. My folks hardly ever come to the synagogue, but they are suddenly adamant that we be married by a rabbi from here. I can't ask Vanessa suddenly to turn away from her upbringing and be married by a rabbi, without her tradition. The fact is that I think her family is much more bound to her church than my family is to their temple—"

"That does not mean your family is not affected by its heritage, just as Vanessa's family rightfully is." I cannot help interrupting him; he is not pleased.

Greg takes a breath. "Rabbi, I—we truly came here for your help. We love each other, but have two different family situations. I don't know how much I owe or do not owe to the Jewish people in how I get married. Vanessa seems to know what she feels regarding her background. One thing I am counting on is the tolerance and the humanity of the Jewish people. If the question offends you, I truly apologize. But I came to ask as your congregant: Will you co-officiate with Vanessa's priest at our wedding in her church?"

"I can't."

But I want to explain why, even as my soul is churning with mixed feelings of sympathy, frustration, concern.

"I can't do that, but I can and will express my hope that you two will find happiness—"

It is too late. Like lithe panthers, they have risen from their chairs, he practically pulling her up. Her hair flies across the edge of my desk as they buck and rear for the doorway. I feel my insides pounding with alarm and helplessness.

Greg stands at the doorway; Vanessa has already vanished out of my sight. His handsome face is contorted and he glowers at me as I sit immobilized.

"I came here seeking some support," he says. "I came here hoping that my people would show compassion. I thought maybe, just maybe, you would see us and hear us and understand. But nothing means anything to you but your high and mighty rules! Instead of making me proud of being a Jew, you embarrass me with your intolerance. So fine, let us be. I don't need you!"

Like a specter, he disappears. I sit at my desk, unable to move. My hands are shaking. I cannot blot out their faces, chiseled by despair, from my mind. *Their love; my responsibilities.* I wanted to tell them so much, and now sit despondent in the utter failure of this meeting.

The door of my study begins slowly to shut. Alice, the religious school director, glances in before closing it all the way, her face a mask of sadness.

CHAPTER ELEVEN

Closed Doors; New Seeds

I SIT behind the closed door of my study for half an hour. As the initial shock of the collapsed interview with the young couple lifts, I find solace in writing down my thoughts for the afternoon funeral of the usher, Abe. I think of the gentleman: He gave me friendship around the synagogue; he was nearly always cheerful in my presence. Now, dear Abe, thinking about you comforts me again. How strange: Writing this eulogy gives me peace in a moment of anguish.

As I run out of written recollections, the real world confronts me again. The office is sealed, the closed door completing the sense of hermetic isolation. I will have to deal with the gaping breach of Greg and Vanessa sometime soon—but after smoldering feelings have a chance to cool. I really have little confidence that much can be done, however.

Meanwhile, the shut door is like the effect of a finger

blister. Mentally pressing against it, I feel both soothed and discomforted. I do not want to go out and do not want to stay in. In the momentary impasse, the memories of other closed doors began to fill my mind.

I saw the bars electronically draw behind me as I walked past the final security check in the federal penitentiary. Lucasville, not far from the river town of Portsmouth, was notorious for its incendiarism, for occasional flare-ups of wholesale violence. Escapes occured not infrequently; the nearby hills of southeastern Ohio were often being combed by armed guards from the maximum security prison. Meanwhile, a lonely convict named Ray had been writing letters to "the rabbi" of the little temple in Portsmouth. Ray, a convicted murderer serving a life sentence, claimed both Jewish descent and the need to talk.

A reliable member of the congregation—a dentist who serviced the prison—confirmed that Ray was Jewish and that he was literate and approachable. "I think you ought to go see him," said the dentist. Stephen— "Dr. Steve"—was a friend of mine. I was very close to his family; he and his wife, Angela, had young children with whom I would endure much.

Steve drove me up to the prison on a Sunday afternoon. He waited in a reception area while two guards escorted me past a series of holding stations. The guards were chipper and pleasant, both young men doing their jobs. "So you're seeing Raymond, eh?" mused one. "He's a live one, all right. Nice fellow, usually. Yeah, keeps asking for a Jewish reverend. You the one he's been writing to?"

"Well," I strove for accuracy, "he's been writing to 'the rabbi' of the temple I serve in Portsmouth. He does not know me, actually. He may know my name by now, but he was just writing to the person he assumed would respond from the temple."

I was very nervous and probably entertained the guards with my flair for the truth.

The bars slammed from behind as we entered a long, gray, cavernous walkway. Truly, I felt that flurry of panic so widely associated with bars shutting in prisons. A final checkpoint. Then, in an ironic burst of pleasant colors and friendly light, we entered a social room complete with tables and vending machines for coffee and snacks. Sunlight came in only from above—through shafts crossed by bars. It was as though I had been admitted to a slanted, surrealist painting. The windows above, the ceilings to the side. Unlike the popular conception, this room had no divider or screen between inmates and their visitors. Men sat, in prison garb, their identifying numerals slapped across the backs. Most of them were joined by a softly speaking friend or relative from the outside; others were waiting. While a handful of the guests were female, the grim, gun-toting guards disallowed any touching. This they enforced just with their eyes.

I was seated across from a skinny, middle-aged man who was shuffling memo-pad paper and snapping a pencil against the table. Ray was busy; he never stopped vibrating throughout my visit. His motions were like staccato bursts of earnestness. He talked to me through long teeth that projected warily from a thin mouth. His words were like breaths of language; he seemed to be jealous of time, even though I knew that time was the one thing Ray had lots of.

"Hello. I thought you wouldn't come."

Was Ray being grateful or cynical? I could not tell. "The dentist told me about you," I said. "I have received some letters at the temple in Portsmouth, and I know that the student rabbi before me also did. Your questions about the Bible and about Talmud are very interesting. You seem to have a background in the Jewish texts."

I was talking about rabbinic literature with a man serving a life sentence for killing a waitress in Toledo.

Ray sat back, sizing me up. He looked like a thin weasel with eyeglasses. His fingers tapped against the yellowish papers; I noticed that his fingernails were long and neglected. It was not pleasant to be with him. Yet it was, I had to admit, rather fascinating.

"Let me show you what I've been thinking," he said. Taking a folded sheet of paper out of the pile, he pointed to a scribbled entry he had headlined DANIEL. "You know, I relate to the prophet."

"Daniel?"

"Indeed." Ray was rubbing his fingers against his upper lip; I thought he would cut himself with his nails. The convict continued: "Daniel said: 'The fear of the Lord is the beginning of knowledge.' "

Daniel of the Bible had not said that; Ray was ascribing one of the biblical proverbs to the Judean exile who saw visions of hope during the Babylonian reign in ancient Palestine. Moreover, Daniel was not really considered a prophet in the biblical canonization. But what was I going to do, correct this individual? His scribbling and his apparent ruminations, sometimes summarized in rambling letters to the generic rabbi of Portsmouth, may have been the saving outlet in his incarceration. So I asked him, "What do you find interesting about Daniel?"

"Well, Rabbi, I find it significant that he's the only one in the Bible to understand that people live after they die."

In fact, the Book of Daniel is the first biblical text to allude to this, although it is a qualified reference, and it is made specifically about those who are either very good or very bad. Ray then accurately quoted from the well-known passage from Daniel: "Many of those that sleep in the dust of the earth will awake."

"Ah, but you didn't finish the verse," I said.

Ray's eyes lit up with interest.

"It goes on, 'Some to eternal life, others to reproaches, to everlasting abhorrence.' You know, Ray, this book about Daniel was used a lot by the rabbis to try and speculate on the arrival of a messiah."

"I know! I know!" The convict was apparently enjoying this sudden discourse very much.

I thought to myself, he might have had a useful life; he really appears to have intelligence and curiosity.

"But the messiah, the messiah really stands for eternal life, no?" Ray's eyes bulged with excitement. In his enthusiasm now, he looked scary to me.

"Yes, in many ways. Everybody has his own ideas. But the Book of Daniel is good food for thought. It set off a great deal of interest in the subject of afterlife. Does that interest you?"

"Interest me? It keeps me going," he said flatly. "It's the only thing that keeps me together."

I was struck by something. "Ray," I inquired, "you are not sentenced to death here. Why are you concerned about life after death?"

The convict smiled at me, and apparently at my youth and inexperience. "I may not get fried, Rabbi. But this is death, being here. A life sentence here is death, my friend."

I noticed that my palms were moist as Ray now rubbed his own hands together with a strange look of satisfaction. Then, with complete accuracy, he pronounced another passage from the Book of Daniel: " 'But you, Daniel, keep the words secret, and seal the book until the time of the end. Many will range far and wide and knowledge will increase.' You see, my friend: Daniel is me; I relate to him. Like Daniel, I need to survive in the lion's den." Then after a pause, he said to me: "You know, I really did kill her."

"I am not asking about it."

"I don't mean to upset you. I just don't want you to wonder about it. Look, I killed her. It was in the back of the restaurant. You may think it sounds pitiful. . . . There was a problem between us. I understood the consequences. I killed her. I used a gun. There was really no court case."

"Were you married to her?"

"I've never been married. But I liked her. We had

161

been friends for a long time. But there was a problem. She just started knowing a lot of things."

"So," I said, fumbling for sagacity, "you've come to terms with it."

Ray smiled, teeth emerging. "Terms? The terms are my life, my friend. I know what my situation is. But I do enjoy the Bible. Can you send me one?"

"They don't give you one?"

"Well, this isn't the Ramada. I asked for one, but they gave me a Christian Bible. It's fine, mostly. But I just would like to have a Jewish one, maybe with Hebrew and English. I can't read the Hebrew, but I'd enjoy looking at it. I asked the dentist, but he said you could send me one."

I shook Ray's unclean hands, feeling the edges of his nails against my skin. I promised him a Bible and mailed one in care of the prison warden the next day. I assume Ray's still there, serving out his life for taking a life, drawing some sense out of the mysterious Hebrew and the quotable English. Surely, a host of other rabbis-in-training have passed through the closing bars, not knowing quite what to expect from the scribbling Jewish inmate who thinks he's Daniel.

Meanwhile, for me and the dentist, there would be yet another set of closed doors.

Stephen and Angela were comfortable in Portsmouth, living in a hilly suburban enclave some distance from the river downtown. He was a man of rugged looks, angular and fit. She was pretty; her face and cheeks round and soft. She was a nurse who had chosen Judaism; they were raising three good-natured children and had always been active in the local, student-led congregation.

I was deeply gratified that the entire family traveled to Cincinnati in June of 1978 to witness my ordination as a rabbi. It culminated a fond two-year relationship which had included the bar mitzvah ceremony of their oldest boy. Their middle child was a girl, Angela's direct reflection. The "baby" was a sweet urchin who bore the same name as me; I affectionately called him Little Ben.

Some time after Cathy and I said a sweet good-bye to the five of them in the summer of 1978, something apparently began to go very wrong for this family. We went to live in Toronto, from time to time recalling our good friends, but not having any direct contact.

The phone call came a year and a half later. It was a neighbor of Dr. Steve's. The worst nightmare of any parent had come true as Little Ben's family found him hanging dead from his own bedpost at home. He was just ten years old. There was another student rabbi already in place in the town, but the family was requesting that I return to officiate at the funeral.

I was terrified. It was not clear to me that I could go through with this; a young suicide is bad enough, but this had personal overtones for me. The utter shock of it (I had seen no symptoms in Ben during my tenure in Portsmouth) seemed potentially overwhelming. In Toronto, I turned for help to my senior colleague at the time, Rabbi Jordan Pearlson. With strong insight, he said to me, calmly and therapeutically, his Boston tones still audible after all the years in Canada: "It's just another funeral. That's how you have to think."

On several occasions since, I have relied upon the same terse but caring intervention to preserve the equilibrium of a colleague in a similar predicament. Of course, when someone a rabbi deeply cares about dies, it is not really "just another funeral," yet it has to be carried out that way. We are the professionals involved; we have to adjust, and make provisions for our grief. This may be accomplished at home, usually late at night, in a sleepless situation, roaming the house. Or, in a classic transfer, it is postponed to the next, less dramatic memorial service. We rabbis say prayers with people; so often, we are articulating our own deferred pain.

Cathy and I flew together, in a cramped commercial prop-jet, from Toronto to Columbus, Ohio—about ninety miles from Portsmouth. Cathy was pregnant with Sari at the time; she stayed with her parents in Columbus while I continued the unhappy journey to the town by the Ohio River.

My father-in-law, his big heart broken by the knowledge of the lost little boy, had lent me his fancy automobile to drive from Columbus to Portsmouth. It was still dark when I set out that morning, and the soft dashboard lights in the heavy car gave me a twinkling measure of comfort. I felt so desperately lonely, making my way in the pre-dawn darkness along U.S. 23, scanning the early sky for the first rays of forgiving sunlight. Why, why had Little Ben done it?

The answer would certainly not come clear to me during the awful weekend I spent with this family.

Vague intimations were made about psychiatric problems that had developed; there was also an apparent obsession with the television miniseries *Holocaust*, which Ben had watched with his family. What was clear to me during the forty-eight hours I spent there was that a mother and father, a brother and sister were suffering and that they would never be the same people again.

Returning from the cemetery where we had just buried the boy, I walked into the family house. It was built against a wooded bluff, handsomely set with long planks, curving balconies, tall country windows. Grief hung from the windowsills and dripped from the flowerpots as I set out for Little Ben's bedroom. I needed some time for myself and felt compelled to spend it in the room which would most recall the boy for me, and where his life ended.

Ben's room, where I had visited him so many times, and even told him a bedtime story or two, was now a frightful sanctuary. It was cluttered with painful memories, laden with abandoned model airplanes, strewn baseball cards, a useless little sock. It was hard for me to stand up; my throat tightened with rich grief. I was also struck by the amount of stereo equipment Little Ben had stacked in his room.

I remembered a conversation I once had with Ben some years before: "I have cable radio, Rabbi!" No doubt Ben had delighted in the reception of faraway stations; he had been an exceptionally curious (but evidently troubled) child, but I can't believe I never saw him troubled. Wiping tears with my handkerchief now, I thought of Little Ben lying there in his bunk bed, listening to the radio with glee, picking up distant baseball games in the summer. I had teased him once, saying: "When I was your age, boy, I listened to baseball in bed, too. But it was on an old, static-filled radio, and all I could do was listen to the local club in Cincinnati. I couldn't plug into the Chicago Cubs or the Atlanta Braves."

"There were no Atlanta Braves when you were my age, Rabbi." I could all but hear his voice now, filled with earnestness and a touch of irony. I looked at the boy's bed, and noticed a set of earphones next to the crumpled pillow.

I walked up to the elaborate stereo system which had been Ben's companion in this room. I pressed the power button and the digital display board lit up. Green indicator lights shone at me. A blast of new-wave rock music shook the room, startling me. With a quivering hand, I pressed the power switch again and ran out.

In the living room, people were pressed against each other, some pouring drinks as they tried to deal with a tragedy that was still bitterly new to them. Steve sat in the corner, his eyes swollen with the salty waters of his unrelenting anguish.

I walked through this parlor, a room thick with sorrow and questions. Ben's father looked at me and we pulled up to each other. His brow was damp with sweat, his lean body appeared limp and broken.

Putting his arm around me, the dentist said: "I don't know why he did it. But I know something was wrong in this house, Rabbi." His voice cracked, and then he said something which I have never forgotten: "My three kids had everything. But I'll tell you something that I realized happened here. I didn't mean for it to happen, I loved the boy so much, but it happened anyway."

My own heart was now melting into my heaving chest as I grasped the shoulder of my friend and onetime congregant. I thought of my wife, Cathy, carrying our own first child; something unbearable was tugging at my shoulder blade. I said to Steve: "Of course you loved Ben. But what do you mean, something happened? Tell me." I was concerned that the poor man was blaming himself, as I have heard so many parents do in the same situation.

"I'll tell you what happened," he continued, sobbing. "They each have everything. They watch their TVs, they play with their calculator toys, they talk on their own telephones, they put in their earphones and listen to God knows what. They each have their own. They each have their own rooms. We wanted to give them their own worlds. So every night my wife and I go into our room, and we shut the door. My little girl shuts her door, the big boy shuts his, and Ben shut his. . . . A big house of doors that are closed shut!"

The father was now crying into my dark suit. "I gave Ben everything he needed to listen to and play with, I ran a cable line in there for him, and he shut his door. We should have been out here in *this* room in the evenings, a family, talking to each other, finding out what was going on—in my little boy's head." The man was inconsolable, and he spoke in gasps: "I'll never know what was troubling him so much because we have been in separate cubicles plugged into our own worlds."

Certainly it was not simply his easy access to an audio terminal or his obsession with video packages that killed Little Ben. There were serious clinical problems at work, and his family had to work very hard together on the road to resuming their lives. I have occasionally seen the other two children in the ensuing years; they have managed to grow and blossom. But the poignant observation of Ben's father that miserable day about closed cubicles has haunted me. Through my career, I have found many manicured, suburban homes serviced by cable lines but devoid of the critical lines of communication among parents and children, siblings and spouses. I will never be sure how culpable Ben's paraphernalia was in the matter of his death; I do know for sure that I retain a certain level of anxiety if my daughters shut their bedroom doors at night. I rest easier if I can hear my babies breathing, or perhaps singing with their radios.

And now, on a Sunday morning at my synagogue, I set aside my memories and quickly go to push open the door of my study. It is time to resume the day; I can no longer bear the feeling of being shut in.

11:35 A.M. A group of eight teenagers are singing the Hebrew lyrics to an Israeli folk song. Their choral poetry draws me into the music room of the school building; it immediately lightens my soul and raises my spirit. *Hinei ma-tov u-ma-nayim, shevet achim gam yachad!* ("Behold, how good it is, for brothers and sisters to dwell together!")

Life dwells again in my body, as songs about Israel and its springtime anniversary bounce against the red-brick walls to the accompaniment of an animated pianist. Nearly breathless with excitement and rhythm, they take a break. The pianist asks me (as I am asked several times a day anywhere in public): "Rabbi, do you have anything to say?"

"Only that you all fill my heart with joy. Your singing lifts me, your faces give me hope. I love you so!"

There is some nervous laughter among the choir students. I have embarrassed them a little. But I don't care. I happen to mean it about gaining cheer from their lyrical expression. Moreover, their music reminds me of the land of Israel—my birth land, and the soil that fostered my father's mulberry tree.

The youngsters continue to stand by. Feeling sentimental, I find myself possessed of the urge to continue talking to them, but I check myself. My brief word of encouragement is enough. The mourning faces of Lewis and Richard, the worried expression of the gentleman with the addicted son, the angry countenances of Greg and Vanessa, the uneasy memory of the prisoner Ray, and the angelic wisp of Little Ben fill my private pockets.

I remember reading in the Bible that when Jacob was troubled about his children, when his heart was full, he nevertheless knew that there is a time for silence. Jacob "kept the matter to himself." So here, now, these children actually lightened my soul; why should I indulge myself on their time? I move on.

CHAPTER TWELVE

"The World Weeps When a Fruit Tree Dies"

T WENTY-EIGHT SAGITTARII is a star in the universe which came into play for earthly skywatchers one July night during a recent summer. The planet Saturn cut across the light of this key star in the Sagittarius constellation; rarely would human beings with telescopes be rewarded with such an astonishing view of the planet's rings and its moons. One of Saturn's moons, the bulky Titan, also obscured the light of the star, further enhancing the remarkable display of Saturn and its offspring.

The galactic revelation, known as an occultation, dazzled astronomers, and it may have tantalized dreamers. But it also served as an auroral statement of faith for people like me: A shaft of light breaks through the blackness, giving life and detail to the handiwork of a creating God. Moreover, if the light can find a single planet from among the infinite ink of outer space, and within the endless ocean of sky, then there is, in nature, the ability of an individual to be recognized by eternity.

The starry phenomenon of Saturn and Sagittarius tells me much as I consider the processes of human memory. The individual soul is incandescent in a spiritual system which believes that God sends out revealing light. The Bible has no doubt that God can focus upon a single human entity; the lighting method used by the deity is remembering.

A grandmother once came to me not long after having lost her husband. I expected her to articulate her loneliness and possibly to bemoan living itself. So often I find myself burying the depressed spouse of an older person within a short time of the first death. In this case, however, the widow came with a different report altogether.

"I am coping!" she told me. "And I have found comfort from, of all places, my little grandson. He came to me last week and asked me: 'Grandma, I can't see Pops anymore, can I?' This upset me at first, as you can imagine. But I answered him, 'No, sweetheart, you can't. Pops is gone.' Then the boy asked me: 'Where is he? Is he in the ground where we went?' Of course, this further upset me, but I was actually glad he was asking the questions. I said, 'Yes, but just his body is in the ground—what he lived in. His soul is somewhere else.' 'Well, I really won't be able to see him then, Grandma. But I do see him, in my mind, every time I just think of him. I see him when I remember him! I guess that way, I'll never really have to say good-bye.' "

The grandmother was filled with pleasure as she

recounted this watershed conversation with her little descendant. She then said to me: "So, can you imagine? Centuries and centuries of religious philosophy and spiritual yearning; my grandson summarizes immortality in one quick conversation! And you know what? He has wisdom. It works for me, too."

When we remember, we give the soul wings. This is a basic Jewish sensibility, and it follows the biblical notion that even God can focus on the essence of a particular individual.

Cast adrift with his family and a host of animals, Noah might surely have felt abandoned and lost. The world had turned into an eternal wash; the horizons offered only seawater and clouds. The story of the dove that appeared with a twig in its beak, thereby signifying land and hope, is widely known. Less known is the biblical verse which, in a more spiritual vein, signaled the end of Noah's isolation: "God remembered Noah." Here is an article of faith: Even if lost, no human being is subject to divine amnesia.

Similarly, God reaches out to a single soul in the story of Sarah. Sarah yearned to conceive a child, even though the years had left her barren. Already discussed here was the story of the three angels who came to Abraham's tent-flap and disclosed the coming birth of Isaac. But the divine signature is perhaps more poignantly inscribed in the nearby verse from Genesis: "And God remembered Sarah." Again, there is a breakthrough, turning light onto the darkness of Sarah's private struggle.

When the great crowds come into the synagogue at

Yom Kippur, they pray for the souls of those who have died before them. The sanctuary is utterly full late in the afternoon of this Atonement Day as the memorial service (*yizkor*) is read and chanted. *Yizkor* means "to remember," but many people mistakenly assume this means *our* memories of the deceased. In fact, the central plea of this dramatic segment of prayers calls for *God* to remember the individuality which was my parent, my sibling, or my child. The fact that we humans remember is a given; why would we be praying if we had forgotten them? Now, looking for reassurance that their souls live on, we actually seek to focus God's attention on their unique and singular qualities. Where do we get such an idea, such a comforting notion, that a deity knows every single human soul? From the reassuring dynamic of a Bible in which God can remember Noah, Sarah, and countless other specific people who specifically needed attention.

If God can remember, we surely can and must. Jews say *kaddish*, a prayer for their dead, at burials, at anniversaries of death, and at the seasonal pilgrimage festivals of the year. The names of deceased relatives are spoken and the prayer uttered. With the name comes the recollection of the face, and then of all those attributes which made that person who he or she was. "I see him and I remember him!" said the grandson of "Pops." Individuality does not dissolve at the point of mortality. This is why so many people now say *kaddish* for the six million Jews who perished two generations ago in Europe's sea of death.

The insanity of the Nazis and their many collaborators swept away towns, households, generations. Little children disappeared in the same maelstrom as their parents and grandparents. Descendants were not left behind to say *kaddish* for the ancestors. This defies the basic Jewish instinct, and the key responsibility the living have to name and pray for their deceased. The technology of the Nazis, which turned genocide into a profit industry, went beyond the physical annihilation of Europe's Jewry (and of several million other peoples, including gypsies, blacks, homosexuals, communists, and sundry "undesirables"). The Nazis reduced many living generations to faceless pulp. No one was left behind to remember the individuals, thereby shrouding their souls with anonymity. This is unacceptable to Jewish history; therefore, in most congregations, the custom is for all to rise and say the memorial prayer—even when we are not recalling a specific relation of our own.

It is a matter of faith for us that if we remember these faceless ones then the God who sends revealing light through the darkest alleys of outer space will restore their names.

But where was God *during* the madness?

This question lives on in the postwar world. It singes the heart as one stands at Yad Vashem, the international museum of the Holocaust in Jerusalem. The terrifying photographs, the wrenching sculptures, the unforgiving poetry and artwork of small children who were interred in the kingdom of death and who somehow still knew to yearn for light. Perhaps most unremitting in the category of horror are the lists: names, names, names. So many names, yet so very few still actually known. The Jews will spend at least another century trying to compile the list of six million names. Meanwhile, we stand and say *kaddish*, entrusting the task of remembering to a deity who seemed strangely absent while the Angel of Death ran rampant from Warsaw to Prague to Paris to Berlin and back. Emerging from Yad Vashem into the crisp sunlight of a free Jerusalem is a kind of Jewish occultation, indeed.

Where was God? The question will not go away, the hollow indictment that offers little satisfaction even to those who want to transfer their anguish into the one source of blame that is as large as the crime itself. The question has endured, even in the housing developments of America where Jews live and shop but are still not spared grief over what happened just fifty years ago.

One of the greatest responsibilities I have ever had was to appear before a group of Holocaust survivors and their children and try to answer the question: Where was God during Auschwitz? Auschwitz, the premier Nazi death camp near Kraków in Poland, has become an emblem for all that is ungodly about this twentieth century. God and Auschwitz: are the terms mutually exclusive? I was one of three Cleveland rabbis asked to testify before the ultimate witnesses in this ongoing trial.

What can a rabbi say in behalf of providence while in a room full of people who literally carry scars from Hitler's death factories? How much does a rabbi really know about God in the context of the Nazi insanity? One is best equipped for this inquiry by confessing up front that the answer is "very little."

Three rabbis—one from each of the major denominations of American Judaism—found relief in each other's presence at a seminar sponsored by a Cleveland survivors' group. The large gathering sat before us with faces that often became strained by a pain and a knowledge the wisest rabbi in the world could never truly assuage.

My two colleagues spoke eloquently and passionately from the contexts of their respective traditions. It was noted that the Conservative rabbi present was born in Germany. I thought: Perhaps there was already a little bit of God working in the sense that such a gathering could hear some Torah taught by a rabbi born in the land of Dachau and the "Final Solution."

This rabbi contended that—painful as it is to acknowledge—Adolf Hitler was a human being, even if he was a monstrous human being. According to Jewish thinking, God installed both evil and good inclinations in humankind; in fact, the two inclinations complete the human character. Evil has prevailed in those who are flawed. Those who are good have learned morality in response to the inherent evil impulses manifest, at some level, in every human being.

The rabbi had properly summarized the Jewish views on good and evil. People are surely a blend of both, and, in fact, the evil inclination informs us about what is good. But had my colleague convinced anybody in that room of Hitler's humanity? I doubted it, even as I felt that the German-born rabbi was making a useful point.

The Orthodox rabbi present was much more declamatory. There is a certain bliss in fundamentalism; there are answers regardless of how difficult the question. The rabbi, literate and aroused about Jewish texts, declared that great lessons are to be learned from the flow of history itself. "Look to our history," he intoned, "and you shall see when we were strong, when we had a community, and when our weaknesses brought us trouble and punishment!

"The holy temple fell in Jerusalem," he shouted, referring to an event of some two thousand years ago, "because we were not united! We did not maintain the laws and rituals! Therefore we lost the ancient sanctuary in Jerusalem! This is a recurring pattern in our history!"

I listened with a mixture of cynicism and wonder. The fiery rabbi proceeded to explain away the pogroms, the expulsions, the turning of supposedly civilized societies upon the Jewish people throughout our history as being the results of Jewish languor. I listened, prepared to dismiss this bit of righteousness, but then I saw that, among some of the forlorn faces in the audience, a measure of reason was actually settling in. Because they had lived through the inversion of logic, this bit of utter piety brought them some relief.

"We must be willing, even at very difficult times, to join in resolve for the law of God!" The Orthodox rabbi had established a rhythm for himself; he was wrapping himself in an imaginary prayer shawl, singing God's praises, bandaging the ills of the world with the fabric of his strict beliefs:

"The *ribbono shel olam*, the master of the universe,

looks down and laments our flouting of his extraordinary gift of this world. No matter what, there is a living God!"

"There is a living God!" The cry went out, with such defiance, such assuredness, that it rang with a certain bittersweet conviction. Surveying utter madness, could a devout person utter anything else?

"But *where* is God?" A wrinkled gentleman, with a strong accent, challenged the panel.

"God is," said the German-born Conservative rabbi, "wherever we let him in."

It was my turn to speak. I rose and asked the gathering what right I had to stand before them. Their eyes gave me no particular response. Here I was, the son of two freedom fighters from Jewish Palestine who had not passed through Europe's long night. I protested my inadequacy to stand up and talk about divinity as against their experiences. Who was I? Parent of two eighties kids who are blessed with personal stereos and carpool arrangements; rabbi and teacher to suburban high schoolers whose idea of suffering is having to write without a personal computer. What could I say about God and Auschwitz?

I begged for their indulgence, however, as I suggested that the question of God's whereabouts in Auschwitz is presumptuous. Yes, the two terms, *God* and *Holocaust*, are mutually exclusive, clearly in favor of evil. To juxtapose these terms implies responsibility—of God—for what happened. Placing God in the death camp in this manner then categorically makes God impotent and the human spirit dead.

I suggested that such a conclusion grants to the Nazi murderers a posthumous victory beyond their ravaging of European Jewry. It also denies the one thing that many of our brothers and sisters had in those camps and gas chambers: God.

I offered, humbly, to the eyewitnesses present (their faces like scorched, fleshy badges) that God *was* there, in the dirtiest, darkest corner of the most horrific barracks, adjacent to the gallows, even as a Jew fell to his knees and for one instant felt the release of prayer.

I reminded my listeners of the stirring courage of those like the late beloved Rabbi Leo Baeck, a concentration camp inmate whose actions accounted for the divine presence even in a satanic place. Baeck, a scholar-rabbi, fussy and resolute, is revered for, among other things, spreading a white tablecloth for the Sabbath in the midst of one of Himmler's barracks.

The two other rabbis listened along with me.

"I was thirteen years old when I came into Auschwitz," said a tall, handsome woman. I shuddered to think how she had survived among the SS. "And I would say to myself all the time, *ani ma-a-mina*, I believe. And I believe in God, Rabbis. We're not all heathens here just because we saw the devil! But I maintain an anger, I must tell you, sirs, against the rabbis from then. The rabbis, they told us not to resist, to cooperate; God would come and deliver us with a miracle. I'm angry they told us to cooperate."

"So what did you do?" The question came back from my Orthodox colleague. For a brief and shrill moment, a look was exchanged between the woman and the rabbi, and I had the unsettling feeling that a scene was being re-created from a terrible flash in the past.

"We died."

Now a gravel-voiced man spoke up. "I was in Treblinka. What God? It's all talk! No one knows. . . . No one understands . . . what we saw, we boys. God? He would have run away from what we had to do, stripping the bodies of everything, teeth, jewels, even hairpieces. No, no one really knows. And let me ask you this: Doesn't this discussion affect every Jew in this city? Is there anybody who shouldn't know exactly what happened? Where are they?"

I sought some insight, some clever way to address this man's blistering despair. But I had none to offer.

Now a woman, probably not as old as her life's experiences made her appear, stood up. "Rabbis, why do I live, and they died? Why am I left to survive? Why?"

A reply came from all three of us, although my throat tightened with a sense of the unyielding grief transmitted by the woman's guttural challenge. As though in final assertion of the point each of us rabbis had come, from disparate interpretations, to agree upon, we all said together, "Only God knows."

The shiny, dark Cadillac, driven by Barnett Bookatz, whisks me from the synagogue to a field of graves. My congregation maintains a mausoleum in our cemetery in which many of our funeral services take place. Now, at 12:30 P.M., in this hall of crypts, I eulogize the very sweet and endearing wife of a large, boisterous fruit salesman who cries in the arms of his two sons. The widower, nicknamed Bull, continues to whisper his wife's name to himself as I speak. "Edna, Edna, Edna, Edna, Edna."

"The world weeps when a fruit tree dies," I say. The phrase is drawn from rabbinical literature and seems appropriate for Mrs. Dubnick. She had been an interesting woman, an avid reader of newspapers, a serious golfer, a sociable and engaging neighbor who enjoyed company around her patio grill. The family lived on the profits of a long-standing fruit concession; they had a fondness for food and celebration and cross-generational reunions. Edna Dubnick was not a historic person; her greatest talent might have been the preparation of her coveted peanut brittle. But, with simplicity and generally kind spirits, she had evidently given her big husband and her two boys much shade and nourishment.

Her granddaughter, Simone, sits quietly and listens as I speak. Simone was confirmed at the temple a year ago. She is elegant and willowy and, though still a teenager, is growing quickly into a young woman. The youngster had worshiped her grandmother, and is now struggling with herself. She wants to cry, but seems bound by the constraints of debutante protocol. The grandmother had knit beautiful wool sweaters for Simone; I now deliberately make reference to this. To my relief, I see a glistening in the girl's eyes as she joins in the growing chorus of sobs.

Simone's soft sounds rise with those of the others, echoing against the high gray walls of this mausoleum. The circular room is filled with souls. The living sit with me in folding chairs, the dead lie inside the walls. I speak from behind a shiny casket, at a marble podium. No microphone is necessary; my voice orbits through the round hall, addressing the spirits. Death has its own building.

The eulogy and prayers are completed. Mrs. Dubnick's generations follow her coffin out of the mausoleum, down the steep front steps, into the field. I am satisfied that the service has had dignity; the silent walk of mourners and friends to the gravesite is actually soothing in the midday light.

I close the rabbi's manual, saying: "May the source of peace send peace to all who mourn, and to all who remember, and bring us comfort as we leave this field bereaved. And may God go with you."

Barnett, standing by, announces with careful solemnity: "This concludes our service. Please allow the family to return to their cars." Then he takes me by the arm. "Let's go. We have two more."

We climb into his car, pulling slowly around the now empty hearse. Barnett makes a call, via his radio transmitter, to the funeral home (base) and to the officer directing traffic at the cemetery gate. Static and voices burst out of the speaker. I think about Bull Dubnick whispering his wife's name while I spoke, and about how very much Hitler had taken away not that long ago.

CHAPTER THIRTEEN

Talking Baseball,
Thinking Justice

ELLIS GARVEY, whom I will now eulogize at 1:30 in the afternoon, loved words, taught the sciences to undergraduates from the world over, was intellectually impeccable, and had died too young, in his fifties. A crowd has formed in the Hillel chapel at the university to recall their teacher and friend. The grief of his widow and her daughter is bitterly compounded here because the family has also lost a young son only months before. The remaining Garveys are burdened with trouble. Here, in a room full of professorial types, I feel that, indeed, the fruit had not ripened.

There was some tension earlier in the week when I met with the Garvey women. In what was a most understandable plea, the mother and daughter had asked me to connect their two losses. Certainly, they hadn't had time yet to finish grieving for the son and brother. And what is enough time? Mrs. Garvey and her daughter (who, thankfully, has a husband and a child) were holding up quite well, I thought—considering the nature of this new tragedy.

But people die individually, and are named individually in the processes of memory. The twentieth century has surely informed the Jewish people about this, and there is redeeming psychological value in this approach. A father's memorial service cannot be a reworking of his son's death; the mind needs to absorb one before the heart can withstand two.

So I resist the impulse to bring the son into the father's requiem, except for a brief requested allusion to the family's stated belief that the two men were now reunited spiritually at the ballpark of the team they both adored. It is springtime, and since Mr. Garvey and his son revered the Cleveland Indians, their spirits are surely hovering over the Indians' training complex in Tucson, Arizona.

It is not for me to question or even wonder at what people in trouble ask me to do. It is for me, however, to try to reflect upon people, in their lives, in facing death, as they are. Besides, this is not the first time that I have dealt with baseball as a therapeutic category in someone's life.

Arlin Schumann depended upon baseball. Arlin was a kidney patient at a facility in Long Island whom I met during my tenure in Bay Shore. It was the summer of 1981—a summer of labor troubles in major-league baseball. Arlin Schumann, in his late fifties, laid up, was nevertheless spirited and chatty, when he could be. Arlin would measure the rhythm of his dialysis treatments against the fluctuations of the baseball standings. While visiting him, I discovered his built-in sense of the present and future by Arlin's daily measurement of "where they stand."

The color gone from his thinning face, the blood being forcefully drained and refilled in his system, Arlin took stock of the world by his regular declaration: "All right. I've gotta check the baseball."

But that summer, the ballplayers struck, and the standings stalled. A horrible inertia permeated the sports pages of Arlin's *Newsday*. Midseason, the cycle of wins and losses, of stats and streaks, simply stopped like a deadened summer breeze. The pumped blood still flowed through Arlin's machine, cleansed and life-sustaining, but it seemed to fade further from the fullness of his cheeks. Some fifty games vanished from the schedule, fifty units of time and space for this downcast fan who could no longer "check the baseball." Indeed, the widow of Lou Gehrig was herself quoted as lamenting "my first summer in fifty years without baseball. It's ruined my summer. I'm just at a loss."

And so I worried about Arlin's spirits: he was like a cast-off kid who could not get into the ballpark. To pass the breach, I began to talk with him about his declared goal of getting to the Baseball Hall of Fame in Cooperstown, New York.

"What a place," he would sigh. "It's been twenty years since I was there. It seems that long ago that there were some real players in the game."

"It is a special place," I said, a serious baseball fan myself. You would think that a rabbi and his ailing congregant were talking about Jerusalem; indeed, a visit to Cooperstown and its popular shrine can be something of the sporting equivalent of a pilgrimage to the Promised Land. Meanwhile, Arlin coped with the pain and the indignities of his infirmity by daydreaming with me about his planned visit to Cooperstown.

His treatments did not affect his memory, or his graceful way of describing things. Substituting baseball lore for present-day reality, Arlin remembered the exploits of Ty Cobb and Hank Greenberg. He daydreamed about Cooperstown and shining Otsego Lake, a long oval mirror that edges along state Route 80, widening its mouth near the baseball village. Arlin described the wooded mountain grounds of the region, tucked far enough away from the New York State Thruway to retain their freshness and their scented seclusion.

I sometimes marvel at the way those who are afflicted in one way seem so resilient in other categories. Arlin's body was failing him; his mind was free and lyrical. As the baseball strike continued, I would sit by his bedside, watching the kidney machines work and listening to his odes to Cooperstown. There in that sterile hospital cubicle, I could see the lake. I could traverse the rich cattle pastures and cornfields along the two-lane highway. I could smell the apple trees and the wildflowers of the valley.

Arlin was dying, but he was passing along his private oral tradition. Mesmerized by his words, I angled across Otsego Lake, past Glimmerglass State Park, and on through Kingfisher Tower, Natty Bumppo's Cave, and Fairy Springs Park. When people are ill, they are still themselves. Arlin had dreams of boating along the Susquehanna River, docking at the Springfield Public Landing, and walking through Cooperstown's Main Street to check out Hank Aaron's 715th home run ball in the Baseball Hall of Fame.

I said to Arlin one day, "You know that Cooperstown has two other important museums, the Farmers' Museum and the Fenimore House?"

Arlin had spoken of the local legends of James Fenimore Cooper's Natty Bumppo character; nevertheless, he responded with a gruff "So what?"

"What do you mean, so what?" I was happy to note his energetic crankiness.

"I mean, so what. I'm glad they're there. But Cooperstown is about baseball, and baseball is the way time is expressed in the summer. That's why this miserable strike makes me so crazy. Who do these guys think they are? If one of these bums makes it to the Hall of Fame, I'll personally see to it that his name is removed. What do they mean, pulling a labor strike like this? Why, the mailmen can't strike, and they walk miles for their wages. These fancy guys, making millions, how can they interrupt something as holy as the summer game?"

Things got a little better for Arlin later that summer, especially after play was resumed in the major leagues. He felt well enough to take strong exception to the divisional play-off system devised to create a World Series champion for that season. "How contrived," he sniffed one afternoon, his nose and mouth under an oxygen mask. "Somebody could win the whole thing without even winning the most games in the full season."

Arlin did not live long enough to see his prophecy come true. He wasn't around to share my indignation that fall when my own Cincinnati Reds, who had won more games than any other team that strange season, failed to qualify for postseason play. This was because they did not happen to win either half of the strike-affected campaign.

And so it was with Arlin. I look for him now each time I visit the baseball shrine in Otsego County. Showing my daughters the lineup card from the spring day in 1974 when Hank Aaron broke Babe Ruth's home run record, I can hear Arlin's anecdotal whispers, his impatient rustling of the newspaper to "check the baseball." I take Sari and Debra upstairs to view Babe Ruth's actual locker from Yankee Stadium. Like an archeological relic, it stands in the center of the hall, surrounded by trophies, uniforms, bats, and other mementos of "No. 3." On the third floor, near "Baseball Cards" and "Evolution of the Uniform," the Sultan of Swat lives on like a sportsman's King Tut.

Along the edges of the exhibits, nice men in shiny red blazers act as guides and storytellers to the visitors in this Hall of Fame. If only Arlin were here, how dashing he would be in one of those sport coats, living out his dream.

I look out into the gathering of mourners at the funeral of Professor Ellis Garvey. It is a diverse crowd, drawn from many of the ethnic textures of America. The students and associates of Ellis were Chinese, English, and Saudi; Jewish and Presbyterian; white and black. He practiced egalitarianism in his responsibilities as a teacher, a citizen, and a Jew. Ellis did not belong to any synagogue. He did not hold deep religious convictions but maintained what he felt was a strong Jewish commitment to the principles of social justice.

Ellis had met his wife, a Hungarian-born woman with a flourishing wit, in a Spanish class when they were both college students. They raised their son and daughter in an open house which was the scene of many civic seminars, cultural events, and neighborhood meetings. People of various creeds would gather on Ellis's front porch to hear his elaborate commentaries on the American electoral system: he lived in fulfillment of Isaiah's ancient admonishment to the Jewish people: "Pray for the welfare of your country."

Surely, like Arlin, he loved baseball, but he loved and appreciated his country even more. I conduct this service, struck by the rare opportunity I have to pronounce Hebrew and Aramaic memorial prayers in front of an eclectic group of Jews, Christians, Muslims, and at least one Buddhist. I see one of the Garvey family friends, a Jew whom I know from the community, weep throughout the eulogy while embracing a similarly upset black gentleman who sits next to him. I quote from a letter once written by Ellis's wife about her husband: "For Ellis, it was always a teaching situation."

When the service is concluded, an honor guard of pallbearers removes the simple casket from the chapel. The faces and hands are yellow, black, and white. Watching this international commitment to the departed

Jew, I think about the troubling disappearance of social action from the agenda of many American synagogues.

Does it require a funeral or a community tragedy to bring together the various cultural groupings of American society? Ellis Garvey certainly created a coalition in the classroom; what parallel patterns remain in the world at large? Even between Jewish groups, there is a nagging enmity. The only time I can recall appearing in a public situation with both a Conservative and an Orthodox rabbi during the last several years was at that symposium of Holocaust survivors. In Toronto, in New York, in Cleveland and elsewhere, the local Board of Rabbis meeting is an assembly of Reform and Conservative rabbis; the Orthodox do not recognize us and they do not sit with us.

I actually can understand the reluctance of a fundamentalist to associate with a liberal or a secular Jew: If an Orthodox Jew acknowledges non-Orthodoxy, then he or she is no longer Orthodox. Piety paints a box. Either you interpret the Bible literally or you do not. There is no gray area (or—I would respectfully submit —opening for human imagination) in the category of fundamentalism. So be it. If the Orthodox Jew is sincere, then I pray that he continues to acquire blissful guidance from his strict interpretation of the biblical and rabbinical literature. The rest of us will continue to work for a spiritual and creative foundation in the real world of mortgages, airline congestion, apartheid, and AIDS.

But meanwhile, there has been a general falling out among American cultural groups that is evident to clergy, and is the topic of much pulpit anxiety. Thanks-

giving weekend produces its annual frenzy of ecumenical services; attendance is not great, and there is a
creeping quality of the perfunctory to it all. My own
concerns here may very well be the product of my high
school legacy: Woodward High School was a long adolescent orientation towards better instincts, even in the
worst of times. It was right, and for me it was *Jewish* to
care about the poor, actually to provide relief to the
hungry and neglected. Coming of age in the 1960s, dealing with the assassinations and with a vulgar, undeclared war brought us fear indeed. But what the best
among us truly feared was the unraveling of a broad
civilization that is as interesting as it is multi-ethnic. We
were also well aware back then that a disproportionate
number of the white folks who were marching against
segregation in Birmingham, Jackson, and Chicago (and
who were maimed and even killed) were Jews; the
Union of American Hebrew Congregations was specifically working in close and caring partnership with Dr.
Martin Luther King, Jr.—a matter of great historical
pride to us forever.

By the mid-1980s, some of the same people who had
marched and prayed and been hosed down in the freedom campaigns of the late 1950s and the 1960s were
wondering out loud what had happened to the spirit of
caring. For a few years before coming to Cleveland, I
worked at the national headquarters of the Union of
American Hebrew Congregations and had the privilege
of day-to-day contact with some of the giants who remain witnesses to what was once a special, even in-
spiring alliance for social justice.

One such individual is Albert Vorspan, the activist who was a key partner of Dr. King's during the days of sit-ins and voting rights marches. We talk frequently about what was and what is; he is concerned about the breakdown between Jews and blacks. There are still good efforts, he claims, but essentially, "we have gone silent."

Vorspan is tall and thin and filled with memories. He seems to be almost an anachronism when he speaks before congregational groups, pleading for a revival of the civil rights movement, for a restoration of dialogue between minority groups. People like him—passionate, stirring, poetic—get together in airport lounges and hotel conference rooms to wax nostalgic about the headier days of the Great Society and the marches on Washington. They knew King, they heard him; they found rich common ground between the way in which the Georgia preacher homiletically rendered an old Negro spiritual and how they recited a biblical psalm. In those days, I suspect, as Debby Siegel and I interpreted our country in the teeming hallways of Woodward, America had a kind of national religion. Its liturgy was freedom, its credo was fairness.

It is not, however, that Albert Vorspan has any illusions as to why the dream has, to some extent, vanished. Like others, he is concerned about those who succeeded Dr. King in leadership roles; a look at the issues of the 1984 and 1988 presidential campaigns reveals the need for a restored dialogue between blacks and Jews. "Not that long ago," Vorspan told me over a late-night cup of coffee in 1986, "we minority groups operated as partners. I recall when Earl Butz said those things about black people. Jesse Jackson and I were on the phone together right away. When any one of our groups was hit, we all got together and made a joint declaration. Well, I tried to get hold of Jesse after that 'Uncle Hymie' thing, and the Louis Farrakhan business. Imagine Farrakhan calling Judaism 'a gutter religion'! Nothing was forthcoming from Jesse. None of the other candidates for president had anything to say about it, either. We Jews were left alone in our hurt. Maybe that's one reason we ourselves have stopped caring about things, although it shouldn't be an excuse."

One of those other candidates for president in 1984 was Walter F. Mondale—whose long-standing friendship with the Jewish people and unswerving support for Israel are matters of record. I met with the former vice president in the fall of 1986, when he was busy practicing law in Washington, D.C. I brought with me the lament of Albert Vorspan about the lethargy in America's social conscience. "Yes," Mondale allowed, "there is a kind of tawdriness out there. People can't be aroused anymore about anybody except themselves."

Mondale, who reminded me that he is "a minister's son," asserted that such things are cyclical. "I regret it's like this now," he said, "but I don't despair. These are the same people who just a few years ago were insisting on all that progressive change."

I had encountered Mondale on a prior occasion—which turned out to be one of the most dramatic in my rabbinic experience. He was not in very good spirits that September morning in 1984, when a group of Jewish leaders were called to Washington to meet with the very beleaguered Democratic presidential nominee. The hotel conference room was crowded and tense. Some polite jokes were told at the dais; Mr. Mondale even found the presence of mind to poke fun at New York's Mayor Edward Koch. Mr. Koch had spent most of his allotted time at the lectern promoting his newly released autobiography, *Mayor*. "I'm certain, Ed, that every word spoken here today will be in the sequel," quipped Walter Mondale. But the gathering that day was ultimately quite humorless.

Mondale then betrayed some bitterness. He criticized Ronald Reagan for having just honored the memory of Mondale's mentor, the late Hubert Humphrey, at a ceremony. "How dare he!" cried the candidate. He proceeded to denounce the president's "hypocrisy." He accused Reagan of "stealing the mantle" from Humphrey. We rabbis and lay leaders in that room were struck by Mondale's indignation, saddened by his evident frustration. The Reagan-Bush campaign hung far away, like a political alpenglow.

Some of the polls at that point were showing Mondale trailing the Republican ticket by as many as thirty points. Mondale's campaign manager, James Johnson, got up before the group and bravely tried to discount the reports. "We're going to turn this around; look for a surprise in November."

This bit of bravado fell like lead into an already downcast meeting. People looked a bit embarrassed. It was an altogether humanizing moment along the heavily programmed campaign trail. At that point, I raised my hand from the audience and asked to speak. My heart was pounding as Mr. Johnson called upon me, and I heard myself saying, "You are talking to a nation that is not listening to you. The campaign is going nowhere, and you are giving us gratuitous sentences." I realized that camera lights were coming on; some men and women with tape recorders and microphones were approaching me. I continued speaking to Mr. Johnson, nevertheless: "You must give us some more concrete and realistic things to take back to our constituents and neighbors."

This exchange was reported the next day in *USA Today*. But Mr. Johnson had promptly closed the meeting just after my little tirade. Walter Mondale, whose eyes met mine squarely for an instant, was whisked away.

Now, in October of 1986, the former vice president smiled at me and said, "I remember that." Now, I was glad to hear of Mondale's good faith in the American people, that we would rebound from our current apathy about social justice. But I pressed him, nonetheless, because of my nagging sense that blacks and whites are indifferent to each other's needs. Why this polarization? I asked the longtime Senate liberal.

"I think there is still a strong residual feeling in white America—with which I strongly disagree—that blacks should be doing more than they are to help themselves, that while the civil rights laws are all right, such things as affirmative action and so on are counterproductive." Mondale stated his admiration for the historical Jewish ability to arrive in immigrant waves, and then, with good educational and family standards, succeed in becoming a signal part of the national fabric. If he was flattering my visit, he nevertheless extended the image to other ethnic groups. "I don't know how many times I've been told, 'Look at the Cubans, look at the Chinese, the Vietnamese. They come in here and they've gotten on their feet. They've got a different color, and we haven't helped them, yet they're part of the American success story.' "

And then Mondale was very emphatic, and he wanted to make sure that I heard him: "This of course—this kind of talk—ignores the impact of slavery, and what two hundred years of discrimination do to a people. It completely overlooks the hard work, the patriotism—in peace and war—of black Americans, their spirituality and decency. It ignores the fact that so many black people have succeeded to the middle class and upper-middle class, thanks to access to college and so on. We have a long way to go, and I would say that there is still that serious and often unexpressed—which makes it more dangerous—sentiment against black people. My God, if you take a poll, certain people won't admit they feel that way, but it's there, in their minds."

I remember talking with Walter Mondale about the state of our country as the pallbearers—Jewish, Baptist, Buddhist—carefully carry the casket of Ellis Garvey to his resting place at Lakeview Cemetery in Cleveland. As always, a fine stillness pervades the scene, the same stillness which has become familiar to me each time I visit another community burial field, Arlington National Cemetery.

I walk over to Arlington almost every time I am in Washington. Arlington was the place I first witnessed —as a ten-year-old in 1963—an interment. My father and mother had just driven up with my little brother and me from a family vacation in the South. I had observed, in western Florida, the exclusion of a young black boy and his father from a gasoline station rest room marked WHITE. Now, passing through the capital, my father had been caught in traffic congestion along Virginia's Washington Memorial Parkway, and we became unwitting witnesses to a military funeral. It was three months before President Kennedy would be buried in this cemetery.

My immigrant father had expressed his discomfort at the gasoline station incident, and now tried to summarize the meaning of Arlington to his two sons. "Here the country honors its soldiers and honors the ideas the soldiers fight for, even die for. Not everything is right yet, it never really gets completely right. But remember that your family chose this country."

It always seems very quiet to me in Washington. The capital is an ironic city of ivory lines and stately contours, framed by frightful neighborhoods of the homeless and distraught. The prevailing stillness is interrupted by the constant drone of aircraft coming across the Potomac from National Airport.

As I pray over the open earth of Ellis Garvey, I also stand in the fields of Arlington. Faces squint at me against the high sunshine of Lakeview, but I hear the muffled drums drifting across the Arlington Memorial Bridge extending from the District of Columbia into Virginia. Caught in recollection, I stand at the grave site of John F. Kennedy, and I remember learning, in a history class at Woodward High School, that the young president once stood at this same spot, beneath the Custis-Lee Mansion, and, struck by the view of the federal city, said: "I could stay here forever."

Nearby, another piece of the collective adolescence I shared with my classmates gone to earth—the simple cross for Senator Robert F. Kennedy. I realize now what it is I feel when in Washington: a kind of loneliness.

A mixed chorus of friends now joins me in reading a transliteration of the ancient *kaddish*; I am back across the Potomac again, to the Lincoln Memorial. Another one martyred; Washington is a village of still monuments for men who died violent deaths. Across the way, 57,000 more epitaphs on a long slab of honor. The Vietnam War Memorial is an extended tyranny of inscriptions written, simply, in the language of names. Close by, another site is charged with memories: the Reflecting Pool, the gathering place of so many demonstrations, protests, and freedom cities.

We shovel dirt into the grave of Ellis Garvey. In spirit I climb up Lincoln's steps. Here stood Dr. King in 1963, the same year of the muffled drums. Here the young preacher invoked his dream. God! They are all so suddenly vanished—here in the Washington of clean monuments and white markers.

The wind blows through the stones of Arlington,

and of Lakeview, carrying echoes of an old oath into my ears:

> I PLEDGE MY HEAD,
> MY HEART, MY HAND,
> AND BID THEE GODSPEED, WOODWARD.

CHAPTER FOURTEEN

When Rabbis Talk to Each Other

ARLIN SCHUMANN, who came to mind this afternoon, would have likely appreciated the irony I now feel—as Barnett Bookatz and I pull away from Lakeview Cemetery and drive off to retrieve my car at the funeral home. It is a few minutes after two o'clock. The irony is that Barnett has entered and departed the cemetery grounds and supervised an interment without the hindrance of lunch hours, labor unions, or long lines. Arlin—the kidney patient who loved baseball—had once alerted me, with his characteristic alacrity, to be on time when I buried him in Long Island. "Otherwise," he chuckled, "you'll have to wait on line, and I won't even give a damn!"

"On line," indeed. Here was a key phrase of my New York years. It did not matter where in New York I was. I came in alone by train or bus; soon I was part of a crowd, invariably waiting "on line" for something.

I often wondered if rabbis in the New York area required some special sensitivity training for the pervasive dynamic of the "on-line" culture: People function differently in the cacophony of taxicabs, talking hustlers, portable radios, pounding feet. Human congestion would move, somehow, against high-rise structures and in between traffic lights regarded more as editorial opinions than as legal facts.

Human souls are more reluctant to surface there in the raging storm of restless traffic, smoking pretzel stands, groaning subway cavities. Arlin had been one of those intrepid commuters for more than thirty years. Each and every morning, he disembarked from a Long Island Rail Road car, disappearing into the swollen repository of Pennsylvania Station. He joined the stampede of attaché cases, newspapers, bagels, coats, hats, umbrellas rushing past tired clocks and overworked muffin stands and exhausted rest rooms into the dim Manhattan light. None of these scores of thousands actually live in New York City; they throng nevertheless into the 32nd–34th Street railroad terminal with bedroom roots in Babylon, L.I., Princeton, N.J., Philadelphia, Pa. Sleeping in the suburbs, working and lunching and straining in the city: No wonder Arlin Schumann had so much to talk about as he summarized his values during those final weeks attached to the dialysis machine. Arlin had stood on one line after another; now he gamely anticipated the ultimate "on-line" experience which he knew was coming: his funeral.

"Be on time," Arlin had joked ruefully. Off the Wellwood exit (#35) of Long Island's Southern State Parkway, in between Farmingdale (#32) and Deer Park (#39), lies one of the greatest concentration of memorial parks anywhere. These include St. Charles Cemetery, Beth Moses, Pinelawn, New Pinelawn, New Montefiore, and others. (Like the living, the dead have also moved out from Queens and Brooklyn to Long Island; thus, the "new" extensions of old burial grounds.) Clergy come from all over the metropolitan area to conduct burial ceremonies in these highly unionized requiem factories. But the clergy know that, unless their party is lucky, they will wait on line at the cemetery. This is particularly and invariably true if the funeral procession should have the misfortune of arriving at Wellwood Avenue just prior to the lunch hour.

It happened to me time and again. If I arrived at about 12:25 P.M. (after an 11:00 funeral service in Manhattan), then the hearse and the grieving family and friends had to pull over, receive a number, and wait. It was so awkward and discomfiting. But it was unavoidable. The gravediggers have their union-mandated lunch at 12:30. We could just sit in our vehicles and sulk. Attempts at conversation with the bereaved, through car windows, were usually futile; there was a desultory feeling about the whole thing. Sooner or later, one or two of the men would climb out of the cars, light up cigarettes, and begin a discourse on the Mets or the stock market. As they flicked ashes onto the lawns, I would gaze across the rows of tombstones, asking God for some kind of insight or explanation for what was actually happening to me; surely this represented some kind of service to the Jewish people which I just failed to discern at the moment.

Finally, a signal was given. Resume the services! But this did not automatically imply movement for me and my party. There were normally two or three funerals ahead of us; at last, we would be able to pull around to a spot which the funeral director had received on a photocopied map from a building in the cemetery marked OFFICE.

Fate was kind on the day we buried dear Arlin. I had lobbied for an early morning service for my box-score-loving congregant. His widow and his children were spared the unseemly wait as we whisked in and out of the memorial field and defied Arlin's many years on line as a New York commuter.

I remember this as Barnett Bookatz now drops me off near my own car on this bright and busy Sunday in Cleveland. Presently there is a little time for myself. I sit in my car, laying the worn rabbi's manual at my side. Lowering the windows to admit some of the mild breeze, I realize that my eyelids sting with midday fatigue. I shut my eyes, letting out a long breath of relief. What a strange and unlikely job I have! I think to myself, as traffic passes along the nearby street. People are coming and going from Sunday picnics, ballgames, rendezvous, shopping trips. Here I am, in dark garb, in between life-cycle events that stop the traffic either at the beginning, the middle, or the end of lives.

Is this what I want to be doing?

I remember a lively conversation I once had with

three of my colleagues several years before, at a regional gathering of rabbis and other Jewish professionals in Southern California. It was after my relatively brief stint in Bay Shore. I was working in the Reform movement and flew out to the meeting in Newport Beach. Visits to the West Coast have been rare for me; it is always a tantalizing occasion for me with my Ohio–Ontario–New York axis. I landed in Los Angeles, eager to experience some professional revitalization in this land that gave us black-and-white cowhide rugs, cotton crewneck sweaters, Giorgio Beverly Hills colognes, spigot-equipped backyard pools, and catalytic converters.

At LAX Airport, I was met by my friend and colleague Allen Kaplan, a director of our movement who serves the New York area. Allen, a worldly, critical, sanguine rabbi who hosts his own religious issues radio program, pulled up to greet me in a rented Japanese car. Feeling as though we had arrived at the other end of the planet, we swung around the ramps and into the rush.

I heard the Chicano rhythms of Los Lobos in the thick highway air as we blended onto I-405, the San Diego Freeway. Pavement everywhere: what a different world for a rabbi to contemplate and interpret. This was not just a road; it was the arterial lifeblood of the motorized metroplex. Having envisioned Southern California as a land of hills and seawater (yielding occasionally to mudslides and brushfires), I was now becoming aware that it is more so a land of ramps, skidmarks, and exhaust trails. The horizon beckoned, but Allen and I could not see it.

"It's a stick shift," bragged my friend, grinding righteously into fifth gear. I looked around at the traffic. The world seemed to be infected with a flurrying virus of Subarus, Hondas, Mazdas, and Nissans. Indeed, Japanese cars buzzed all about, as though they had been catapulted in collective Nipponese airstreams directly from Kyoto. This was Los Angeles, where I discovered that even the anchorwoman on the local CBS affiliate was named Toyota.

The sun was setting into Pacific waters that evening as I gazed out at Catalina Island from my hotel room in Newport Beach. Allen and I were joining two other colleagues and heading through Hollywood to Spago, the landmark eatery and social vortex. Leonard, a local rabbi from Santa Monica, provided the transportation in his car—a Toyota Corolla. The fourth partner was Ronald, a Jewish camp director from Indiana.

At the restaurant, we sat at a circular table—four religious professionals amidst the trendy and celebrated. Off in the corner, silhouetted against a bay window, the starlet Morgan Fairchild looked out into space. No one joined her or even spoke to her during the two hours or so of our visit to this *ristorante*. If Miss Fairchild wanted privacy, we rabbis wanted pizza.

Allen, who in another life could be the social critic for a prominent northeastern magazine, commented on our surroundings: "This place is good, but people who are really hungry eat first."

"You're never satisfied," grumbled Ron.

"He knows what's good," I defended my longtime friend.

"He loves saying it's bad," shot back the camp director. "I go with him to restaurants when I'm in New York. If he doesn't like it, it's not just bad, it's *baaaaad*."

It is true about Allen Kaplan, a thoughtful and discriminating denizen of Manhattan who once made me walk thirty blocks on a Friday afternoon to get just the right sweet challah bread from a tiny German bakery he particularly admired. Allen sat now in Spago and hummed a little of Giacomo Puccini's *Tosca* to himself. He had just seen the opera at Lincoln Center. "This is the way people should live!" Allen raved about the experience to us. "We walked over to the opera house, and for fifteen dollars my wife and I sat way, way up in the stratosphere. But who cared? It was beautiful! You could hear everything. That's the thing about New York. Everybody has access to the greatest art and music in the world. No wonder the Jews came in and fell in love with the city."

"So what do you think about Los Angeles?" asked Leonard.

"It's baaaaad."

We all laughed.

Allen, who might be described as a hybrid of Woody Allen and the prophet Samuel, dismissed all of us with a quizzical look. It was as if to ask: Isn't what I have to say obviously true? Allen is a rabbi to rabbis, in his capacity as a regional director of the national organization of Reform congregations. He loves to claim disdain for the congregational rabbinate ("Who needs to listen to people's problems all day?") but, in fact, his work with rabbis and synagogue leadership serves to

ameliorate the day-to-day functioning of religious insti-
tutions.

Rabbis and their congregants often misunderstand
or misinterpret one another. A rabbi can make a single
enemy in a congregation and thereby run a risk to his
very security—and that of his children. A rabbi can often
learn something about a congregant which the congregant may later regret or resent having the rabbi know.
There is fertile soil in congregational work for the growth
of thorny stocks. In any case, we rabbis carry secrets in
the linings of our dark suits; sooner or later we are called
to task.

When rabbis get into trouble, they turn to other rabbis. Generally, these adviser-colleagues are the ones
working in a capacity such as Allen's. Not necessarily
always equipped with the answers, they at least offer
the safety valve of confidentiality and the relief of sympathy. There are certain things rabbis understand together about the incongruities of human life that rabbis
cannot truly commiserate about with lay people. Is there
a veil between rabbis and lay people? Yes, to some extent. Maybe it's because rabbis are the ones who, in a
grocery store or at a ballgame, cannot completely relax
in the sudden company of a congregant. Having buried
somebody's parent, and having that same person sit on
a board of trustees that determines your income, can
you really be casual at the check-out counter with him
or her? Are rabbis ever afforded the luxury of anonymity, of having not to be "on"? That only comes in the
separate company of other rabbis, who are living
through the same syndrome, and whose spouses and

children are also marked for public discussion in the local community. Perhaps only another rabbi can understand: Our congregants, with whom we pass through just about everything imaginable, yield us the greatest joy but can also deliver the most staggering hurt.

My friend Allen has worked both in the congregational and in the "administrative" settings. I envy his versatility. He is totally comfortable with being "the rabbi" whether he is teaching a conversion course at a local synagogue or he is making elaborate hotel arrangements for the next convention of his synagogue region. I think we like each other because we are both pretty much at peace with how the rabbinical elements of our personal lives coexist with our mutual desires to be fathers, husbands, theatergoers, baseball fans, epicureans, and libertarians. While Allen may sometimes sniff at the entanglements of pulpit life, he has little to apologize for in the category of human services: He was stopping in Los Angeles, upon this occasion, prior to boarding an aircraft carrier anchored off San Diego. My friend is also a veteran navy chaplain who specializes in the nonsectarian treatment of alcoholics and substance abusers.

Ronald, the camp director, never even attempted pulpit life. Altogether suited for his work, Ronald began running his summer program while still in rabbinical school. Ron is most happy in cut-off jeans and a Chicago Cubs cap, romping through the humid Indiana air, leading and organizing his counselors and staff in the care of their young charges. Ron directs a facility that offers a curriculum in Jewish communal life in the summer while functioning as a study and seminar institute during the other seasons of the year.

I suspect that Ron, whom I worked with while a rabbinical student, may never leave his duffel bag behind and enter the more formal world of congregational life. He is not ambivalent about it, saying, "That's not for me. Camp is my life. I'll leave the pulpit to you guys." Ron's definition of himself is not at all unique in North America. Only about half of those ordained to the Reform rabbinate actually serve in congregations. The rest are camp directors, educators, psychologists, publishers, administrators, or directors of community agencies. We also have a handful of graduates who are happily selling jewelry, practicing law, or running the family business. Meanwhile, Ron lends his presence as "the rabbi" to the business of maintaining his summer community. I don't know if he would be comfortable handling some of the specific situations I deal with in hospitals, funeral chapels, and board rooms, and I know I lack the patience or commitment to tour congregations in the winter with camp slide show and pitch, or to handle a broken bone or a bruised ego with the insights Ron brings to the hot days of summer.

Leonard, who rounded out our pizza-seeking foursome at Spago, was perhaps the one rabbi in the group who had not yet found a niche. Brilliant, contemplative, utterly Californian in orientation, Leonard came from a long line of medical professionals. He had excelled at the University of Southern California in physiology and now brooded as the rabbi of a modest congregation in

Santa Monica. I often wondered why Leonard hadn't become a physician. The rabbinate sometimes attracts unlikely candidates; it can seduce and then confound good people who really have a sincere spiritual quality but lack the disposition for the day-to-day realities of the clergy. You may serve God in this profession; you're much busier servicing people and their egos. I hurt for my colleagues who thought that there weren't politics in the pulpit. They are often crushed or humiliated in this field—especially in big, urban congregations which are maintained by successful, impatient people who need a rabbi to be as savvy as he or she is pious. They want prayer, but they demand common sense just as much. Naïveté and simplicity may be good for heaven, but a knack for problem solving and a politic, even wary, instinct do better for rabbis while making progress on earth.

Do I denigrate the rabbinate by saying this? Absolutely not! No one loves its complicated, sifting, illuminating aspects more than me. I just do not suppose than any job is done well while operating with illusions. Leonard is a delicate, fascinating man who knows more solid rabbinical text than I know baseball statistics. He can repeat Talmudic dissertation with breathtaking accuracy. But he does not know how to engage his congregants. He gets angry when they tell him they would like him to dress less casually at their family functions; he recoils at small talk and is unable to mask his sometimes churning moods in the face of a congregational event that requires him to be in good cheer. What's Leonard guilty of? Nothing, except being himself. Unfortunately, the contemporary rabbinate requires the suppression of self in favor of public perception. Rarely are we rabbis of the American culture accepted purely for our scholarship or our devotions. We are ministering to a society which is purchase-oriented, consumer-centered, business-minded, recreation-obsessed, life-style-packaged. Certainly, we had better know how to pray; we must believe in God; and we must maintain the standards of the rabbinical and biblical literature. To be otherwise is to become invisible in a civilization which floats on superficiality. But, on the other hand, we are not the ancient priests of Judea. We are not the village scholars of Gdansk or Bratislava. We are the rabbis of Shaker Heights, Fort Lauderdale, Tarzana, and Short Hills.

I confess to feeling that rabbis spend too much time waiting for "holy moments" to happen. By this I do not mean to remove holiness from its transcendent quality; the Jewish word for holiness, *kedushah*, actually means "separation." When two people are married, or when a group of people are truly moved by prayer, or when a child is named—these are moments of utter holiness, separate from the more mundane experiences of humankind. But perhaps rabbis try too hard to be ready for such flashes of opportunity, and miss the less obvious but potentially satisfying glimpses of human contact. Not everything that has happened to me in the realm of inspiration has occurred in or around a synagogue building.

I wish to remind the reader of my friend Laurie Beechman, the actress I referred to earlier. Chanteuse, sculptress, worldling, Laurie is one of those people who fulfills the Jewish sensibility that God is most creative through the skills and efforts of his human partners. Laurie is the soulmate of my family, Cathy's Broadway consort, a role model and cheerful emblem of achievement to my daughters. Such an association is not unique in the world; what I hold precious here is that this relationship is the unlikely outcome of a simple note dropped in the mail.

Laurie won professional prizes for her leading role in the New York musical *Joseph and the Amazing Technicolor Dreamcoat*. It was in this production that I first saw her in early 1982. I accompanied a temple youth group to this realization of the poignant Bible story of Joseph and his troubled brothers. The story line may have yielded a challenging set of lyrics for Laurie and the cast. It happens to be a haunting, revealing lesson in sibling rivalry and family tension for people like me who view the Bible as a psychology manual. The young singer narrated the plot with a rich voice, expressive eyes, and good spirits. Returning home from the Royale Theater, I wrote the actress a note, thanking her for her performance.

To my surprise and delight, a handwritten response came not too long afterwards. The actress expressed her appreciation for my sentiments, and encouraged me to follow her career. This was all I needed; within a few weeks Cathy and I were in the audience, joining a theater full of admirers who had also come to hear the newly nominated candidate for a Tony Award. We knocked

on the starlet's backstage door following the performance.

"So *you're* the rabbi?!" Laurie Beechman, still tow-
eling her hair dry in her dressing room, enjoyed my
informal Sunday-afternoon dungarees. Cathy and I
were probably younger than she had imagined. At any
rate, a friendship was immediately born and has continued through the years via correspondence, telephon-
ing, and many happy reunions. About the jeans she
beheld on a visiting rabbi that first Sunday, the actress
had exclaimed, "Wait till I tell my grandmother!"

Many visits and one year later, I ran into Laurie in
the lobby of New York's St. Regis-Sheraton Hotel. She
was performing there in a revue. She looked wan and
weary. What was the matter? She told me that her
grandmother had died; I now understood better the apparent bonding between the woman and her ancestor.
Laurie suddenly became less the New York talent and
more the sorrowing granddaughter. She was suffering
from some doubts about faith. There was little I could
offer as solace except to listen. But that she related to
me now as a rabbi moved me and endowed me with a
responsibility that I regard as the unique by-product of
my profession.

Laurie spent the middle years of the 1980s singing
the keynote song, "Memory," in Broadway's *Cats*.
Cathy, my daughters, and I moved on to Cleveland, but
the connection between us only strengthened with the
distance. It would be oversimplifying the friendship to
suggest that it is a long-running song and dance. Like

anybody, Laurie has weathered personal crises and professional setbacks, though not at the expense of her resilient faith and spirituality.

There is a photograph, much cherished in my family, of a group of people in a living room with all the folks in the picture wearing odd hats. Two little boys, Laurie Beechman's nephews, and two little girls, my daughters, smile away, framed by my Cathy, Laurie's sister and brother-in-law, her mother, and her stepfather. What had begun as a postal exchange between myself and the actress was now fulfilled seven and a half years later in a Philadelphia parlor. The two families had just met each other that same evening, and now, before parting company, we had donned hats from Laurie's mother's extensive collection of theater artifacts for a frolicsome snapshot. There was much emotion in the air. This long-contemplated get-together had been prompted by Laurie's recovery from a serious illness. Indeed, the stage door had now been opened all the way. Laurie, preparing for her next show, wrote a letter to my daughter Sari that transmitted her satisfaction about this completed circle, and her relief that "God has been good to me."

I believe that God is especially good to all of us when individuals and families find each other in the common cause of human caring. The friendship between Laurie and myself may very well have occurred anyway. But, inasmuch as it was her profession that sparked it, it is mine that gave it a framework and the means to extend it. Time and again, my vocation has been a fortunate passport with which to present myself. Above all, I am grateful that being a rabbi gives me the access to hold other people's souls in trust.

I rub my eyes and sit up straight in my automobile. The sun is hanging directly across the horizon; it is nearly 3:00 in the afternoon. Turning the engine over, I check to make sure that the rabbi's manual is in the seat next to me. In a few minutes, I am driving through the peaceful field of flowers and carved stones. It is my second visit to Mayfield Cemetery this long Sunday, and it is time to bury the usher Abe.

In the open-air tent, Barnett Bookatz stands with Abe's son, Lewis and Richard, and their wives, Janis and Leah. They look fairly relaxed and at peace. The widow, Florence, has been placed in a cloth seat near the exposed crypt. She stares directly at the regal oak box, which shines in the light like a fallen but restored tree trunk. I join these familiar people as the rest of the crowd of some sixty people, including Abe's grandchildren, takes seats or places in and around the tent. The ground has been opened, but, it seems to me, it does not cry out in pain here. This family has lived and died well, with dignity.

At the makeshift podium, I remember Abe and the gentle greeting he brought to our congregants as they entered the sanctuary.

"A rabbi may fairly ask and realize," I say to the gathering, "how such a smile and such a genuine demeanor has helped two generations of Jews enter the synagogue at the threshold of prayer. They came to meditate and to remember, to perhaps listen to what a rabbi had to say. But I sense that they were first—and most fortunately—affected by the eager, urbane welcome they received from this committed, groomed gentleman. Abe was my congregant indeed; I remember him as a *mensch*. . . . We are grateful for Abe—a friend who lived long, lived warmly, with devotion, and who made a temperamental century a little more delicate. . . . Give him now the fruits of his work; his life itself proclaims his praise."

Perhaps the most meaningful moment beside a grave site is the period of silence. The wind whispers through tent flaps. I think of Abraham of the Bible, sitting by his own doorway, the desert wind bringing him insights and messages. The real eulogies are written across the heart. The silence is deep, mystifying, rich with gratitude, regrets, promises, and, always, secrets. I think of the telling passage from Deuteronomy, when the retiring Moses attempts to comfort the people about matters that lay, unresolved, like stones in the soul: "The secret things belong to God," says the old teacher. So be it. Whatever else it does, the Jewish tradition attempts to fill the corners of our tents with peace.

Voices then join with me: "The Lord is my shepherd; I shall not want. He maketh me to lie down in green pastures: he leadeth me beside the still waters. He restoreth my soul. . . . Yea, though I walk through the valley of the shadow of death, I will fear no evil, for

Thou art with me; Thy rod and Thy staff, they comfort me. . . . Surely goodness and mercy shall follow me all the days of my life: and I will dwell in the house of the Lord for ever."

After burying Abe, I return to his home with his generations. I conduct a brief memorial service and ask his sons to light a seven-day candle. The burning light is symbolic; the Jews believe that the flame, like God's lamp, represents the human soul.

Then we break bread together, a ritual that takes place regardless of the time of day, upon returning home from a burial. My tradition believes strongly that the living must go on living; thus the immediate impulse in favor of nourishment. Moreover, sitting and eating following the prayers and the lighting of the memory candle is a first act toward resuming normalcy.

In more traditional times and places, friends and neighbors prepare this "meal of consolation." Now, the customs of grief are usually augmented by delivered condolence "trays" from selected delicatessens. Nevertheless, the ritual at home, which sets off several days of receiving and remembering, is useful and soothing, and it offers the possibility for quiet empathy.

Abe was a lovely man. Leaving his house, receiving the thanks of his widow and his children and grandchildren, I suddenly feel something stirring in me. The enforced public isolation of my professional life has been broken. I enter my car, and, trying to put the key into the ignition slot, feel my throat tightening. I see my own father; I see my little brother and me standing over his open grave. I almost manage to stifle a guttural release, but part of it breaks through across the dashboard of my indifferent Pontiac.

Trying to push out the thoughts of my dead father, I drive off to my 5:30 wedding.

CHAPTER FIFTEEN

"With This Ring Be Thou Consecrated to Me"

B UT it is not so easy to shut out the thoughts of my father. I am asked often enough: "Tell me, Rabbi, was your father a rabbi?"

He was not; Jeff Kamin was a mechanical engineer, an amateur soccer star, an aspiring Hebrew poet, and an emigrant from Israel to America. I have tried to imagine what he might have been like as a grandfather, and how he might have related to a son who preaches about human life from a Midwestern pulpit. My father was part of that young group which literally founded the modern state of Israel. He was eighteen at the time of Israel's Independence War, and he received shrapnel to his eye from a Jordanian attack. He also lost virtually his entire circle of boyhood chums. They were wiped out by an Arab Legion ambush while my father slept. He was on an assigned leave, and rested under the mulberry tree in the village of Kfar-Saba. This was a nap from which I believe my father never truly woke up; the incident may explain his lifelong tendency to periods of melancholy.

I keep two of his prizes in a special drawer. There is a pullover sweater with his athletic letter *M*, won at the Colorado School of Mines, and a medal from the Israel Defense Forces for heroic conduct under fire. My father quoted from the prophets, and he cherished a handwritten letter he once received from David Ben-Gurion.

I sometimes find it hard to believe that my father, who dodged bullets in Palestine, and who helped smuggle used Nazi machine guns (still embossed with swastikas) into the new Israel from Czechoslovakia, should have died while playing handball in a Cincinnati gymnasium. When people come to me with similar incongruities, I know that my soul gives them answers that my brain may not.

Like many contemporary Israelis, my father prayed without any particular institutional format. He loved traditional Judaism but was not necessarily ritualistic. I do not think instinctively of my father when I walk into a synagogue; he comes to mind more readily when I visit at the edge of New York Harbor and stare at the lapping waves.

From time to time, I visit these waters, knowing that, floating somewhere in this bay, is a droplet of salty water which I claim surreptitiously for myself. It was the teardrop of my father, who wept into the bay one sunny morning in 1962.

That watershed day marked the return of my father

and mother to the United States, and their landing as immigrants. We were standing in brilliant light aboard the *S.S. Israel*, two weeks after having left the port of Haifa. It was before the World Trade Center was built, but Manhattan's skyline still brimmed with an immense power for a nine-year-old boy. My little brother Sam, then three years old, was connected to my mother on the deck by a straining child's leash. But as I would see, something in my father was coming quite unleashed.

He had first arrived here in 1954 as Ze'ev Kamin; he had already renamed himself with the more American "Jeff" by the time he collected his family and went back to Israel in 1961. On board the *S.S. Zion* on that journey was Jeff Kamin's 1957 Chevy Belair. The white sedan with its shiny red interior was also returning to New York Harbor on this bright spring morning in 1962.

My father, strong and bulky, could never get over the taste of American chocolate bars. The confectionery of American life was too sweet, too satisfying for this large man who made up his mind that the United States was for him. But it was more than the candy bars: The processes of democracy and of an open landscape tantalized the onetime defender of Israel's narrow frontiers. I can recall my parents' breathless all-night vigil around the tiny black-and-white television set in November of 1960. A small, political group of Israelis and Europeans joined them as they awaited the news of John Kennedy's election to the presidency. It was important to these immigrants and foreign exchange students. If the young Catholic senator could make it, then minority people like them could conceivably dream bigger dreams in

America. (Many years later, my father ran in a local primary as a designated delegate for the presidential campaign of Senator Henry "Scoop" Jackson. Though the senator lost the primary election, my father's hands-on appreciation of the American political system was never lost upon his children.)

Proud, curly-haired, my swarthy father now stood at attention in New York Harbor. His sinewy arms grasped the railings of the ship as I stood and watched him. Normally given to conversation, my father was quiet. Other parents and children walked by chatting nervously; seagulls danced in welcome overhead. But for me, there was no sound, as two images came into focus.

The large stone face first came to me through the upper strands of my father's thick, windswept locks. I did not know Lady Liberty would be there, "a mighty woman with a torch." After these fourteen days at sea, at close quarters with the shrill excitement of my young parents, the view of the greeting colossus was at once frightening and sublime.

I stood in my father's shadow as our ship steamed past. He had been staring at the statue, not at the skyline of the looming city. A single tear glistened across his left cheek. Sea spray, the statue, the harbor, and my father's own single drop of salty water were converging for me into an indelible and precious memory of coming home. I saw the drop fall into the waters as my father turned towards me.

He spoke in English that was peppered with Semitic inflections: "My son, she is the statue to America. She tells us we have arrived." I recall the somewhat strange sense that my father had been engaged in a dialogue with the 105-foot lady he had been waiting for since the day this ship had departed Haifa.

Whenever I return to the edge of these waters, I recall my father and the manner in which he embraced his new country. I can still hear his voice reciting the Bill of Rights to himself. I see myself, in a Cincinnati court-house, standing alongside him as he swore to preserve those principles.

When I pronounced the oath of citizenship—there with him—I also swallowed down subliminal doubts about really "belonging." My juvenile sensibilities made me feel that I would not be a part of the mainstream U.S.A. My parents, after all, had strong accents and foreign-looking friends. Our apartment neighbors were not the directors of the local PTA. Rather, they gathered together and formed cultural societies, drinking Turkish coffee, reviewing books or playing canasta while exchanging anecdotes and opinions in Hebrew or Yiddish or Russian.

Alongside the bay waters, my face refreshed occasionally by salty splashes, my rabbinate is reinvigorated with strong images. My parents' story has yielded memories and associations for me more normally retained by people who were passing through places like Ellis Island when my own parents were still children in the British Mandate of Palestine. I look at Sari and Debra now— the granddaughters my enigmatic father never saw— content in the knowledge that my generations have passed, with meaning, from a holy country to a remarkable land. I serve a mainstream congregation, grateful that the rabbinate bridges these two worlds. Perhaps I have found what my father scanned the horizon for that sunny morning. Nevertheless, it is my rabbinate which connects the mulberry tree of then to the Astroturf of now.

A bride and groom wait for me at the synagogue's urban location. This is our main temple, not the branch—where I began the day. The chapel of this round Byzantine structure is simple, with fine pews and stained glass recalling the ancient tribes of Israel. As I enter the building, the best man, an affable sort, sees me and announces to anyone within earshot: "He's here!" And to me, he says, "Nice wedding suit, Rabbi."

I am feeling a little tired, and momentarily grouchy, and respond cryptically, "It works as funeral suit too, babe."

But the evident bloom of the bridegroom and bride soon cheers me, and serves to whisk away the residual effects of death and dying. These two, Mindy and Jimmy, have impressed me in our previous meetings with their friendship for each other and their instincts one for the other. Mindy, a very beautiful bride, greets me in her ivory gown, her doelike eyes sending out messages of hope and life.

The bride and groom, along with their parents, and the three surviving grandparents, follow me into my study. Marriage documents are signed; there is the bureaucratic license from the state, and a *ketubah* with our congregational logo. I explain to the family that the word printed across the top of this Jewish marriage contract is *kiddushin*—which means "holy matrimony." I ask the bride and groom to touch the document, signifying their acceptance of its rather simple conditions: The bride and groom should love each other and look after one another as beloved friends.

The room begins to fill with emotion. I have left the cemeteries far behind now and feel a thick sense of privilege here. These two children are passionate about each other and evidently are in great need of each other. I tell them now: "The way you feel about each other is the way God felt when he made the world in the first place. I am so sure you will be good for each other! You truly fulfill what our tradition tells us, that God makes new worlds constantly by causing marriages to take place." Now I ask Mindy, whose oval face is glowing with optimism: "Can you sit down? We want to make a fuss over you. In spite of everything being said about making men and women the same, today is the day for a bride. Indulge me a moment. The love you feel is as old as time."

Mindy happily accommodates me, getting help from the others with her long dress. Jimmy stands next to her; I am beginning to really enjoy how he can't take his eyes away from her.

"Now, dear family," I say, "I want you to look at your son and daughter. Your children are going to the wedding canopy! Just a moment ago, it seems, you held them in your arms, now they have arrived to be married. Surely you have something—each and every one of you—to say to both of them. Grandparents first, one by one: Come forward and place your hands on the faces of these children, and give them your blessing. It can be out loud, whispered, or even unspoken. Take your time, step forward."

Another wave of emotion comes now; feelings and mascara run. There is a kind of hush-toned break-through: A group of normally restrained, elegantly polished suburbanites suddenly discovers a gratifying release of caring tension.

Jimmy's grandmother takes Mindy's cheeks in her wrinkly hands and does not let go. "*Oy, a sheine meidele!* You beautiful girl! Does my grandson know what he is getting? You should grow old with him, in comfort and joy! Jimmy! Jimmele!" The grandmother's hands now squeeze Jimmy's face as though it were a sheet of challah dough to be kneaded. "Jimmele! Your grandfather is looking down on you, and he knows what's happening here. I can feel his arms around me because of what is happening here. Oy, thank God I lived to see this day. My Jimmele! My boy!"

"Okay, Ma, take it easy." It is Jimmy's mother. "Ma, you'll ruin your eye shadow."

"Big deal." The grandmother is not going to let her daughter's embarrassed anxiety affect her own ability to celebrate the coming full of her generations.

"I didn't know about this," Mindy's mother makes an appeal to me as she keeps adjusting her makeup. Nonetheless, what she says to her daughter in this session could only be expressed by a mother who once carried this grown-up child inside her womb.

Mindy trembles behind her veil now, her eyes like salty pinwheels dropping water across the front of her dress. The parents, grandparents, and I suddenly realize that we are all watching the same thing: Jimmy wipes away Mindy's tears with such tenderness that I begin to wonder if the world could possibly embrace such uncompromising sympathy.

Now I address Jimmy and remind him that the biblical Jacob arrived at his wedding canopy looking for his inamorata, Rachel, but instead he found Rachel's sister, Leah. He had to work seven more years before he could marry the woman he wanted. "Look now into the eyes of your bride, Jimmy. If she is the right one, then give her your blessing."

Jimmy, looking virtually dry-cleaned in a stiff tuxedo, finds the face of his betrothed behind the white lace.

"You're just everything, Mindy."

The public wedding ceremony a few minutes later is almost anticlimactic. I was convinced of the sincerity of this young couple back in my study. Now, under the canopy, Mindy and Jimmy are like two handsome figurines escaped from a wedding cake. But I am sure that the session of spontaneous private blessings has given this somewhat choreographed ritual a little more incandescence. I require that a bride bring candlesticks handed over by her mother or grandmother and that a groom provide a family wine goblet for the wedding ceremony. The tapers lit, the light reflecting against the silver cup, the man and woman exchange rings: "With this ring, be thou consecrated to me. . . ."

If the two people love each other, as is the case here, then I leave the canopy touched by the exalted sense that we all had just glimpsed the light of creation.

After the wedding, Mindy's mother asks me to join the family at their reception, which promises to unfold soon at a nearby club with flowing wines, live musicians, excitable aunts and uncles, mood-changing light shows. "Bring your lovely wife," the mother adds, genuinely.

I rarely attend these post-wedding or post–bar mitzvah festivals of roast beef, Dauphinoise potato, steamed asparagus, and assorted tortes. They take up a lot of time and are a potential threat to my cholesterol count. But I have stood by, on occasion, somewhat awestruck by the opulence of such gatherings. Sipping from a tall crystal glass of champagne (in which floats a perfect little raspberry), engaging in polite talk with cigar-smoking older men whose sons are in the process of taking over the business, I often wonder what my ancestors in old Palestine might have thought. Certainly, the gnawing feelings of inadequacy that I carried in my early years in this country are long vanished. Not only am I a part of the mainstream, I serve its professional and business vanguard. Here I am, dodging overflowing plates of sturgeon, brushing past the musk-scented characters of the post-*shtetl* American success story: The men are urbane, manicured, coiffured; the women, like sports cars, are imperially slim, tucked, frosted. I look after them and their children at their life-moments of holiness. I find, regardless of how prosperous they may be, that they are interested in and intrigued with this sacred intervention from the traditions of the Jewish people. But on this Sunday afternoon I offer my regrets to Mindy's mother. I realize also how much I have missed "my lovely wife" through the course of the day. I have not seen Cathy and my two little daughters since the morning. Indeed, my heart aches to draw my girls close after I put down the phone, now back in my study at the temple. A young mother has phoned: "I heard that you were doing the Richschaefer wedding, so I thought I could reach you." The woman tells me that her eleven-year-old daughter is hospitalized with a severe pain in her knee. The doctors have told the family that it could be a tumor; they will know more early tomorrow.

"Is your husband there with you?"

"We're separated. But he's flying in. It's okay, my parents are here. Randi is in good spirits. I just wanted you to know. Maybe you can stop by." The mother's voice cracks across the cold phone lines.

I make a quick decision about going to the hospital right now, and hope it is all right. "Let me stop by tomorrow morning, after they do the test. I'm sure I will be more helpful to you and Randi then. I just wanted to make sure you two are not alone."

There is a pause on the line. I pray the mother will agree; my own emotions are now bare threads, and I honestly believe she may need me more tomorrow. To my relief, she says, "Well, then, you're not so worried, are you?"

"I don't worry until I have a reason, love."

"Will she be okay?"

"She *is* okay. She's the best. This kid will deal with anything, I know it. I'll check on you both tomorrow. Meanwhile, God be with you. Let me talk to Randi."

"She's sleeping, Rabbi."

"Let her sleep. You are tired too, I'm sure. Rest. The whole world is tired. Tomorrow may be filled with hope."

As I walk out of the synagogue, a few stragglers from the wedding pass me by. Their laughter falls hollow against my troubled soul. Suddenly, I remember the time when I thought for sure that I was about to lose my Cathy.

CHAPTER SIXTEEN

Still Light in the Sky

I T WAS several years ago, just months after our younger daughter, Debra, was born. When I walked toward our porch and saw her face, I knew there was trouble. The fumes from the departing taxicab hung in the warm air; it was late in the day, and Cathy's face was drawn. Pale light and vague fears filled the yard as my wife spoke to me: "I am sick. I have a problem." It was only then that I realized that she was holding little Debra. I had only seen Cathy's countenance from the curb to the front steps. Her green eyes tear-stained, she put down the child and buried her face in my shoulder. I stroked my wife's blondish hair.

I did not understand: A few moments before, I had been a restless commuter and my only concern was the train's exasperating tardiness. Now, rail timetables and the day's office gossip evaporated into a kind of murky steam. The intrusion was out of step with the way we live together. Cathy and I speak on the phone together ten times a day. We know everything about each other. Well into the second decade of a marriage, we have never even considered the ethos of reappraisals and creating spaces. We're old friends, and ours is the language of private verifications and big plans. That she heard from the physician while I was trapped on a recalcitrant train from New York and thereby had to agonize alone for an hour was a violation of all our basic patterns.

The doctor had, in fact, called to report on the results of Cathy's recent physical. She had been given a sonogram, ostensibly to check her gallbladder. The doctor indicated that the gallbladder was fine. However, a "mass" was clearly visible on my wife's liver. She must see a specialist immediately.

God in heaven—this was not supposed to happen to us. I'm the rabbi; people in this kind of trouble call *me*. I give them a measure of empathy. Who would be *our* rabbi?

My wife is an easygoing young woman who rarely enjoys a glass of wine, does not smoke, and has a very hearty laugh. What kind of arbitrary attack was this on a good-natured household with a keen sense of generations and a nicely maintained station wagon? There would now pass a period of three weeks in which two people would discover the ultimate meaning of mingling souls, of living literally on the cusp of tears and relief.

The first news was altogether disheartening. The specialist who saw Cathy's sonogram required her admittance to the hospital immediately for the painful ordeal of an arteriogram. She was considered to have a tumor which was the manifestation of a rare condition known as liver cell adenoma.

The doctors involved tried, with compassion, to hide their fascination. This is a circumstance which affects only one woman in 500,000. Somehow I knew that the operation they recommended had a certain allure for the doctors because Cathy's predicament was so unique. I felt the doctors' awkward blend of concern and professional interest—not without some bitterness.

In the years since then, I have attempted further to examine this visceral reaction on the part of some to the clinical intervention of medical professionals. There are certainly things that I, in my work as a rabbi, have found as interesting as the individuals or families involved have found terrifying. A remarkable and insightful general practitioner in Cleveland lunches with me often. Dr. Hadley Morgenstern-Clarren and I have found many ways with which to bridge the parallel experiences of rabbis and physicians. Hadley reads Maimonides, the medieval Jewish philosopher-rabbi-doctor. I listen as my friend grieves over losing a patient or celebrates the successful treatment of another. It turns out that clerics and medics are often applying different kinds of tourniquets to the same family; it behooves me to learn much more about the emotionally braided world of the doctor.

Meanwhile, I agonized for my wife as the doctors injected dyes into her bloodstream. I thought, what was there for a radiographic picture to realize but the soft colors of her sweet soul? The diagnosis of adenoma brought with it some consolation, for the doctors asserted that, while dangerous, it generally was under-stood to be a benign kind of growth.

But our luck was qualified. Cathy's tumor was evi-dently located high up and in back of her liver. The medical team *had* to operate in order to really ascertain Cathy's status. The location of the mass made the sur-gery complicated and risky. Then came the word: It was possible that malignant cells lined the walls of this spot in Cathy's young body.

She was told this by her physician. He told her and then left her alone in her hospital room. I arrived ten minutes later, having brought our daughters to the care of that afternoon's baby-sitter. Cathy—who a day earlier had calmly prescribed for me the nature of her funeral —now conveyed this information to me. Fear gripped our fingertips as we held on to each other. My life's mate remained composed. I wondered how little I knew about her even as I felt I knew everything. Meanwhile, it was time to begin questioning all of it. But first, it was time for me to cry.

I told Cathy I wanted a soda but went to the tele-phone booth downstairs in the hospital foyer. When does a grown man call his mother long distance? When he needs money? When he is afraid his wife might die? My mother's voice broke my chest. I pounded the walls of the little booth, my tears splattering the glass doors. I gasped in throttled bursts of childlike horror. The chain broke, and the book that held the yellow pages crashed to the floor. All the questions and the anger about what is fair and not fair poured into the indifferent receiver.

At that moment, I was no rabbi; I was a scared son and husband. My mother listened, sobbing in response to this telecommunicated bit of a nightmare. I prayed for my little girls, who had only begun to know their mother.

Cathy was released a day later. The operation would be scheduled in the near future. We had two medical opinions which confirmed the need for the surgery. But now I began a rampage—and became at the same time enlightened and tolerant of families in similar crises who also insist on turning over every medical stone before conceding a loved one is lost.

Reminding the doctors that they themselves had contemplated the possible effects of the use of contraceptives upon liver coloration, I insisted upon further diagnostic exploration. Some months before, Cathy had been treated for an episode of gynecological bleeding with megadoses of formidable contraceptive pills. Cathy and I now began to agree that her body would not again be indiscriminately given over to medical procedures.

Sometimes people make decisions together which are as fateful as they are indicative of the nature of a relationship. Such moments of sealing the heart occur around the breakfast table, in bed at night, or along a pathway somewhere. My wife and I walked along a mountain trail at Grossinger's, the erstwhile resort hotel in New York's Catskill Mountains. It was just a few days after the portentous reports of the doctors, and we had halfheartedly signed in as delegates to that year's national convention of Reform rabbis. Allen Kaplan was there, and other dear acquaintances. But we kept our secret to ourselves for the time being, and existed in our cubicle of mutual support.

We walked now, holding hands and fingers. Cathy said, "So what should I do?"

"We don't give in, that's what. Cathy, I just feel that you are all right. I just feel it. They are wrong, and you do not have to give them your body to satisfy their medical curiosity." My defiance was truly not an act to inflate my beloved's confidence; I took her hand, gazed at the ring with which she had consecrated herself to me, and said, "I was very frightened at first, there is no question. But, somehow, something tells me you are not sick! I am going to work on the doctors until they can find a second or a third opinion which confirms this. Baby, don't let them cut you up for nothing."

"All right, I won't."

Working generously with me, our doctor tracked down a renowned expert in the study of liver-related arteriograms. The gentleman taught at Emory University. We phoned down to Atlanta. Could the specialist read Cathy Kamin's chart? Yes, he probably could, except that he was spending time on leave in England.

My local doctor felt the fury breaking out of me: "So get him over there! Send him the pictures! Please!"

We persisted, and waited. We went through the motions of everyday life, focusing on the trivialities of disposable diapers, the newspapers, baseball scores, lawn mowing, housekeeping. We rented movies on the secondhand VCR I had recently purchased; they provided mild distraction. We took drives in the car, not hearing the music that played on the radio, given to long silences during which our souls swam together in prayer and in love.

I began to consider the effect of all this upon my existence as a rabbi. Cathy did not expect me to be "the rabbi" with her. Her green eyes shone on me with her always simple expectation that I should be myself. I did not consider what life might be without her, probably because it was too frightening an option. I had already been with people in pastoral situations when I had to tell them that they were, in fact, going to die. I was, and remain, a believer in this approach to the denial of a congregant that he or she is terminally ill. I am convinced that, once the individual is through being angry with me for saying it, he and his family may then begin the urgent process of closure. It is not always the right approach, but when it seems necessary, this kind of frankness usually does help a situation.

I wondered, could I ever be so forthright with Cathy? With myself? The rabbinate seemed to give me insight about everybody's crises except my own. But then a strange but vaguely soothing realization came over me: If it came to that, it would be Cathy herself who would, by virtue of being herself, somehow guide and mitigate the situation. This lesson sustains me now through every crisis I face or encounter: Such a time brings the nature of a person to the surface. Sometimes you are strong; sometimes they are stronger. Cathy, in trouble, honed my instincts.

The phone rang one day: The diagnosis was apparently wrong! The "mass" was, in fact, a great discoloration (something known as hemangioma) and not liver cell adenoma. The doctor in England had sent back the wonderful word; one glance at Cathy's personal map and he knew. Withhold the knife! The tumor was altogether an innocuous spot on the arteriographic record. Our prayerful hunch on the cumulative effect of the administered birth control pills was validated.

Much time has now passed. Cathy submits annually to precautionary CAT scans. The emotional wounds have faded, but never the sense of what might have been. We have buried other members of our extended family. The cycle of grief comes to us now with more informed concern. Old friends—we look at each other now and know a lot. And again, I feel blessed to work in a profession where experience yields on-the-job wisdom.

Tomorrow does bring hope quite often, even to a working world fraught with the frailties and ailments of human life. In the rabbinate, human life triumphs in both its endings and its beginnings. Though I fear it as I drive away from my round synagogue late on a Sunday afternoon, it turns out that there will not be trouble for the little girl named Randi. After the removal of a benign growth in her knee, the sprightly youngster will adjust to life with crutches for six weeks.

Now evening is coming: Three people have finished their lives, two others have exchanged wedding vows, a host of schoolchildren have prayed and sung, a young couple has bristled in frustration over the conflict of their faiths in the midst of their love. A father has coped with the pain of a son lost to addiction, two brothers have found common ground in recalling their generations. Mothers and fathers, children and parents, living and dying. The soul is filled with stones; only some dissolve.

There is still light in the sky as I reach my doorstep. I have had even longer days, indeed. My own love stands and greets me. My children come running. I embrace the flesh of my flesh, the lives of my life. My eyes blur with salty waters. Then we all break out laughing as my older daughter says to me: "Daddy, I never want to be a rabbi. Don't you do anything all day but talk to people?"

About the Author

B EN K AMIN was born in Kfar-Saba, Israel, in 1953 and raised in Denver and Cincinnati. Following ordination from the Hebrew Union College in 1978, he served pulpits in Toronto, Canada, and Bay Shore, New York. Beginning in 1982, Kamin served three years in New York City as North American director of the World Union for Progressive Judaism, the international agency of Reform Judaism. Kamin now serves as senior rabbi of The Temple–Tifereth Israel in Cleveland, Ohio, where he lives with his wife and two daughters.

Temple Israel

Minneapolis, Minnesota

IN MEMORY OF
BEATRICE GROSS
FROM
MR. & MRS. EDWIN HARRIS